A BOOK OF PRAYERS

*A Guide to Public
and Personal Intercession*

ARTHUR A. R. NELSON

IVP Books

An imprint of InterVarsity Press
Downers Grove, Illinois

InterVarsity Press
P.O. Box 1400, Downers Grove, IL 60515-1426
World Wide Web: www.ivpress.com
E-mail: email@ivpress.com

InterVarsity Press® is the book-publishing division of InterVarsity Christian Fellowship/USA®, a movement of students and faculty active on campus at hundreds of universities, colleges and schools of nursing in the United States of America, and a member movement of the International Fellowship of Evangelical Students. For information about local and regional activities, write Public Relations Dept., InterVarsity Christian Fellowship/USA, 6400 Schroeder Rd., P.O. Box 7895, Madison, WI 53707-7895, or visit the IVCF website at <www.intervarsity.org>.

Scripture quotations marked NRSV are from the New Revised Standard Version of the Bible, copyright 1989 by the Division of Christian Education of the National Council of the Churches of Christ in the USA. Used by permission. All rights reserved.

Scripture quotations marked NIV are taken from the Holy Bible, New International Version®. NIV®. Copyright ©1973, 1978, 1984 by International Bible Society. Used by permission of Zondervan Publishing House. All rights reserved.

Scripture quotations marked The Message are from The Message. Copyright © 1993, 1994, 1995. Used by permission of NavPress Publishing Group. All rights reserved.

Permission for the excerpt from Guerillas of Grace by Ted Loder, ©1984, 2005, admin Augsburg Fortress. Reproduced by permission.

Permissions for excerpts from God Is a Verb! granted by the author Merilee Zdnek.

"When Grief Is Raw": Words: Brian Wren, © 1983 Hope Publishing Company, Carol Stream, Ill. All rights reserved. Used by permission.

Prayers from Before the Amen, Maren C. Tirabassi & Maria I. Tirabassi, editors. © 2007 The Pilgrim Press. All rights reserved. Used by permission.

Prayers from Blessed by the Presence of God by F. Russell Mitman. © 2007 The Pilgrim Press. All rights reserved. Used by permission.

Prayers from Hear Our Prayer by Glen Rainsley. © 1996 The Pilgrim Press. All rights reserved. Used by permission.

Design: Cindy Kiple
Interior design: Beth Hagenberg
Images: leather texture: © rusm/iStockphoto
cross: © JipJip.com/iStockphoto

ISBN 978-0-8308-5736-4

Printed in the United States of America ∞

Library of Congress Cataloging-in-Publication Data

Nelson, Arthur A. R.
 A book of prayers: a guide to public and personal intercession / Arthur A.R. Nelson.
  p. cm.
 Includes bibliographical references.
 ISBN 978-0-8308-5736-4 (pbk. : alk. paper)
 1. Prayers. I. Title.
 BV245.N45 2012
 242'.8—dc23

                                                    2012038469

| P | 19 | 18 | 17 | 16 | 15 | 14 | 13 | 12 | 11 | 10 | 9 | 8 | 7 | 6 | 5 | 4 | 3 | 2 | 1 |
| Y | 28 | 27 | 26 | 25 | 24 | 23 | 22 | 21 | 20 | 19 | 18 | 17 | 16 | 15 | 14 | 13 | 12 |

CONTENTS

INTRODUCTION

Scripture calls us to pray for one another—and promises the presence of the Spirit in the midst of our prayer. However, when people are presented with a specific situation of emergency, be it physical pain, a difficult relationship or grief in the midst of loss, words for prayer do not come easily. During my five decades in pastoral ministry, I have found that in times of pain (or even of celebration), I have yearned to have at my disposal words that speak appropriately to the heart. I have imagined a collection in a form small enough to carry from place to place at a moment's notice, and not so cumbersome as to appear to symbolize another burden in the face of a situation calling more for sensitivity than overpowering presence.

In these pages you will find *A Book of Prayers*. Most writings are my own, which I offer in humble gratitude to God for whatever freshness comes as you read and pray. When I have added the writings, here and there, of authors who have especially touched my life, they are clearly credited in the notes and on the copyright page. The book is divided into the following sections for ease in finding the right words at the right moment:

Praying the Inner Life. Often when we are carrying the burden of others' needs and hopes and the compelling issues of our larger worlds, we are aware most of our own inner hungers. The prayers in this section are intended to speak to the heart with an openness that liberates and encourages both wrestling and courage.

Prayers for Times of Grief. The prayers here offered are intended to be quite specific. They address those moments in our lives when words do not form easily because of the surprise or pain we are encountering. Let them become catalysts for your own sense of freedom in approaching God on behalf of yourself and others.

Prayers for Times of Difficulty. There are stress-points in our lives that arouse in us reactions that both deeply unsettle and surprise us. These unsettling occasions uncover a wide range of discoveries about ourselves—resentments, anger, fear and much more. We need prayers that help us to be free and honest before God in these times.

Prayers for Ongoing Illness. When illness is diagnosed as chronic, the lives and plans of both the affected ones and their caregivers are dramatically changed. Phrases like "how long?" have the ring of despair and uncertainty. Family tensions and misunderstandings may arise. Clear prayer-words can ease the way.

Prayers for Healing. Often our prayers for healing center on physical ailments and emergencies that have immediate visibility and what we perceive to be the best way for the Spirit to restore. For those ailments that are more hidden, like old memories that are not pleasant and sleepless nights, pray in confidence that God understands and welcomes our open conversations.

Prayers for a Marriage. These prayers are offered with the recognition that even "good" marriages are an adventure in growth, progress and promise. The challenge to keep relationships strong, the intrusions of misunderstanding, even fractures in the wedding promises, are a human reality. Some are healed Some are not. And the fallout hurts in many ways. Use these prayers for your own situation and those of others in your circle of care.

Prayers for Parents and Children. Who could adequately address the many challenges of parenting and child-raising? To draw on the continuing and faithful ministry of the Holy Spirit through prayer welcomes strength beyond our own. With the Spirit's discernment, many of these specific areas will yield the fear and uncertainty to the comfort of being held in the midst of so much that demands the parenting of children, young people and even our aging elders.

Prayer for Celebration. Praise and thanksgiving to God, that we have been given much to celebrate in our personal and common life. Here are just a few. Count your own blessings, add a prayer of your own for how good God is in the routines and emergencies of your life.

Prayers for Home and Church. These prayers help us to "get ready" to enter worship. Then they can assist us as we carry our Spirit-life back home, formalizing the blessing God intends for us. We remember to sit at the table with prayers on our lips for what is prepared at this moment for us—nourishment, food, drink, good conversations.

Praying for Our Larger World. These prayers are offered for times when public emergencies and local and national celebrations call for corporate petition, intercession and thanksgiving.

Praying for the Year's Seasons. Changes in the climate and atmosphere of our natural world and the transitions in the liturgical year are opportunities for acknowledging the power and nurture that accompany them. Here you will find resources for praise and thanksgiving for what God creates and sustains, for the liturgical year, for the turn of the seasons, for whatever nourishes the wondrous moods of our lives.

Praying the Scriptures. Because many people have found the Scriptures to be our great consistent source of comfort, strength and peace, praying with them has historic precedent. My hope and prayer is that those biblical treasures will continue to fill our prayer experiences and yours.

As you begin to explore the other offerings of the

book, perhaps it will become a resource for you, a new milepost for a long tradition of a prayerful life for years to come.

All of this would not have come to fruition were it not for outstanding preparation and editing gifts of a dear friend, Fern Katter. Sincere gratitude to her and the strong and sensitive support and encouragement of Cindy Bunch at InterVarsity Press.

ARTHUR A. R. NELSON

Praying

the

Inner Life

Touch Me Deeply so That I Will Find a Sense of Self

O Ingenious God,
I rejoice in your creation,
and pray that your Spirit touch me so deeply
that I will find a sense of self
    which makes me glad to be who I am
        and yet restless
            at being anything less
                than I can become.
Make me simple enough
    not to be confused by disappointments,

clear enough
    not to mistake busyness for freedom,
honest enough
    not to expect truth to be painless,
brave enough
    not to sing all my songs in private,
compassionate enough
    to get in trouble,
humble enough
    to admit trouble and seek help,
joyful enough
    to celebrate all of it,
        myself and others and you
through Jesus Christ our Lord.

Guide Me into an Unclenched Moment

Gentle me,
Holy One,
into an unclenched moment,
    a deep breath,
        a letting go
            of heavy expectancies,
                of shriveling anxieties,
                    of dead certainties,
that, softened by the silence,
    surrounded by the light,
        and open to the mystery,

I may be found by wholeness,
    upheld by the unfathomable,
        entranced by the simple,
            and filled with the joy
                that is you.

I Need to Breathe Deeply

Eternal Friend,
grant me an ease
to breathe deeply of this moment,
    this light,
        this miracle of now.
Beneath the din and fury
    of great movements
        and harsh news
            and urgent crises,
make me attentive still
    to good news,
    to small occasions,
        and the grace of what is possible
            for me to be,
                to do,
                    to give,
                        to receive,
that I may miss neither my neighbor's gift
    nor my enemy's need.

Precious Lord,
grant me
a sense of humor
    that adds perspective to compassion,
gratitude
    that adds persistence to courage,
quietness of spirit
    that adds irrepressibility to hope,
openness of mind
    that adds surprise to joy;
that with gladness of heart
I may link arm and aim
with the One who saw signs of your kingdom
    in salt and yeast,
        pearls and seeds,
            travelers and tax collectors,
                sowers and harlots,
                    foreigners and fishermen,
and who opens my eyes with these signs
    and my ears with the summons
        to follow to something more
            of justice and joy.

It Would Be Easier to Pray if I Were Clear

O Eternal One,
it would be easier for me to pray
    if I were clear

and of a single mind and a pure heart;
   if I could be done hiding from myself
      and from you, even in my prayers.
But, I am who I am,
   mixture of motives and excuses,
      blur of memories,
         quiver of hopes.
knot of fear,
   tangle of confusion,
      and restless with love,
         for love.
I wander somewhere between
   gratitude and grievance,
      wonder and routine,
         high resolve and undone dreams,
            generous impulses and unpaid
            bills.
Come, find me, Lord.
Be with me exactly as I am.
Help me find me, Lord.
   Help me accept what I am,
      so I can begin to be yours.
Make of me something small enough to
      snuggle,
   young enough to question,
      simple enough to giggle,
         old enough to forget,

foolish enough to act for peace;
skeptical enough to doubt
the sufficiency of anything but you,
and attentive enough to listen
as you call me out of the tomb of my
timidity
into the chancy glory of my possibilities
and the power of your presence.

Grant Me an Enchantment of Heart

O God of children and clowns,
as well as martyrs and bishops,
somehow you always seem to tumble
a jester or two of light
through the cracks of my proud defense
into the shadows of my sober piety.
Grant me, now, an enchantment of heart
that, for a moment,
the calliope of your kingdom
may entice my spirit,
laughing,
out of my sulky self-preoccupations
into a childlike delight
in the sounds and silences
that hum of grace;
so I may learn again
that life is never quite as serious as I suppose,

yet more precious than I dare take for
    granted,
  even for a moment;
that I may be released
  into the possibilities of the immediate,
and rush,
    smudge souled as I am,
      to join the parade of undamned fools
        who see the ridiculous in the sublime,
          the sublime in the ridiculous;
and so dare to take pratfalls for love,
  walk tightropes for justice,
    tame lions for peace,
and rejoice to travel light,
  knowing there is little I have or need
    except my brothers and sisters to love,
      you to trust,
        and your stars to follow home.

Prayers for Times of Grief

When Grief Is Raw

When grief is raw and music goes unheard,
and thought is numb, we have no polished
      phrases to recite.
In Christ we come to hear the old familiar
      words:
"I am the resurrection. I am life."

God, give us time for gratitude and tears,
and make us free to grieve, remember, honor,
      and delight.
Let love be strong to bear regrets and banish fears:
"I am the resurrection. I am life."

The height and breadth of all that love
      prepares

soar out of time, beyond our speculation and
our sight.
The cross remains to ground the promise that
it bears:
"I am the resurrection. I am life."

All shall be judged, the greatest and the least,
and all beloved, till every hurt is healed, all
wrong set right.
In bread and wine we taste the great home-
coming feast,
and in the midst of death we are in life.

Naming a Stillborn Child

Well-loved child, nurtured for many months in *his/
her* mother's deepest warmth, our sorrow in knowing *he/she* cannot sustain life in this world loses
some of its sting in knowing that *he/she* returns to
your eternal home and your boundless love.

It is comforting now to name *him/her*
_____ _____, a name drawn from our weeks of
anticipation of *his/her* arrival and from hearts and
minds that somehow sensed _____ was,
and will continue to be, a significant part of the
beautiful tapestry of our lives.

And as we release _____ to resurrection living with you, help us all be reminded that even our deepest losses are redeemed, and that by the mystery of your ways with us, our mourning will ultimately be turned to joy.

Farewell to a Newborn Child

God of all days both glorious and heartbreaking, it is on this heartbreaking day that we pray for an unusual gift of comfort and strength. For today, _____, this tiny child who will not get to know the delight of this world, has died.

_____ and _____ have embraced this child with the miracle of birth and graced family in heart and mind only to be asked to carry the grief that has come with this devastating disappointment. Bless them in their grief with the knowledge of your grieving heart as well.

On the Death of a Loved One

Understanding and loving God, we admit today that our grief hurts because we have lost a significant part of our own lives that we will miss deeply.

We also are feeling guilty, in a way, that when we

had the chance, we didn't support more, share more, even love more. We console ourselves a little in the knowledge we didn't know more or understand more, but we still would love to undo our neglect and our insensitivity.

So we pray that you will take away our guilt by the strength of your great forgiving grace. Perhaps then we might be able to focus more on the wonderful life of _____, whom we have lost, than on whatever selfishness there is in our attention to our inadequacies.

On the Anniversary of a Suicide

Continue to hold us, O God, still struggling to comprehend how and why _____, whom we loved dearly and still do, took *his/her* own life. On this anniversary of that day of raw grief and sharp pain of mind and spirit, we remember with deep gratitude how you came alongside us with both comfort and strength clearly not our own.

Now we ask that you keep ministering to us when at unshielded moments we continue to feel the anger of the hurt, the waste, and the self-accusations of not being able to help prevent the tragedy. Make us increasingly tenderhearted and compassionate, as you have been with us, and keep reminding us that neither _____ nor we are out of your sight and mercy.

For One Who Has Been Raped

Comforting God, the word that comes to me over and over again is "violated," that is, the strong and frightful feeling that does not go away.

The help I plead for is to be released from the feeling that my body, my life, has been spoiled. I don't feel safe and I am fearful where I had no fear before.

My emotions swing from anger to grief, to rage and bitterness, and I have this feeling that I need to be mended, that I am not clean.

By the wonder of your Holy Spirit, breathe on me the assurance that I am defended, that you can lift me out of my many wounds of body and soul, and that soon I will feel whole and free again by the miracle of your love and grace.

On the Death of a Pet

Understanding God, you know what our pet _____ has meant to us. You know because in your creative genius you give us pets for us to enjoy and love, just like the first days of record in the Bible. We believe that dogs and cats, rabbits and turtles, fish and birds and lots of other creatures teach us lessons about loving and receiving love, often when those lessons are hard to find and learn in other places.

Now _____ has died, and although we have been doing our best with the veterinarian to keep _____ healthy, nothing in our power could keep this from happening. Now, God, you who love every one of your creatures, hold a wonderful place for _____.

And bless all animal lovers everywhere. Surround them with your love in memory of all their much-loved pets.

Prayers for Times of Difficulty

For One Moving to Retirement Living

Companion God, you who have been attentive while
_____ has been sorting and distributing
treasures of the home in preparation for this moving
day, keep holding *him/her* in your embrace until *he/
she* settles into *his/her* new environment. It is a huge
change for _____ and for us, too. We're
exhausted by the work of transition and the emotional realities of saying farewell to place and life-
long comforts.

May _____ find __[new home]__ a
place of easy friendships and spiritual warmth, as well
as a fresh kind of joy and a place of new securities.

A Caretaking Spouse's Prayer

I want to be honest with you, God, when I say that I really want to do my best in caring for _____ with the full measure of love in my heart.

I also want to tell you that a lot of the time I am tired, disagreeable, impatient and spiritually dry, and I don't like myself for feeling like this. I sometimes resent that I must now provide the support for family and realize that my dreams for our relationship will never come true as _____ and I had hoped.

Give me a new and understanding spirit along with strength to endure. Let me see _____ as you do and perhaps be so filled with that measure of love that I can endure and know again both hope and joy.

For Those Who Have Been Robbed

Righteous God, coming home today, we have been enraged to find the doors damaged by forced entry, the rooms so upset and possessions so tossed about, that our hearts grieve with the loss of both treasured things and precious memories.

Much stolen can never be replaced, but grant us the reminder that justice belongs to you, that we may be given the ability to surrender what we have lost, and to give thanks that you will give again both possessions and meaningful remembrances appropriate to our life together and with you.

To Cast Out Fear

Merciful God, the night, the next turbulent storm, the next doctor's report and the flight across the country are real threats often enough. To believe in despair that we all live in a fearful world is yet another thing altogether.

In either case, to be preoccupied with fear's hold on my life moves me to pray the more that this darkness I find in so many places will yield to the light of your Spirit's presence and promise that I am not alone, that when you say, "Fear not," it means that you are holding me close and that this enemy fear is not too much for you or for me.

For One Under Financial Stress

Lord, few things challenge my patience and my inner unsettledness like financial worries. Part of the preoccupations they foster is due to both tight budget and also the call to sound stewardship.

I resent the power of money to control my thoughts and time. I am sometimes obsessed with scrambling for more sources of income while reluctant to stop buying more than I need. Frequently my preoccupation with financial balance is in conflict with those nearest and dearest to me and the tension fuels strain at home.

So my prayer is for your help to give me strength and courage to choose wisely and spend responsibly, and to be patient and understanding with those who are keenly connected to the outcomes in our mutual goals.

For One Being Bullied

Tender and loving God, my heart is deeply touched on hearing that _____ has been the object of hateful and relentless fun-making and brutal emotional abuse. Give _____ today a new assurance that your compassion is stronger than the taunting and that *he/she* is fully loved and accepted by you just as *he/she* is, full of your best gifts for *his/her* life.

May *he/she* also know that you understand completely the anger and humiliation that have taken occupancy in *his/her* soul, and that your love and peace transcend everything that arises in the face of such difficult and hurtful happenings.

For the Unemployed

Now out of work, God, I'm bothered deeply with anxiety, causing confusion and sorrow. I am sometimes uncomfortable pretending well-being when I am torn up inside, even hiding from family and friends.

Lacking the security of being gainfully employed is undermining my confidence in being both good provider and good person.

Help me, God, to believe in myself, to be aware that you are in my empty and unsteady place with me, guaranteeing my worth and supporting my prayers for fulfilling work and for feeling whole again.

For the Unemployed

Creator God, after your six days of vigorous, fruitful and all-encompassing creation of the world, you showed us by your own design that rest from labor is a great gift. Praise to you for the marvel of sabbath.

But our thoughts reach out to those who don't have the work to rest from, and what should be rest is, rather, anxiety and grief.

Help us not to make so much of our own fortunate labor that we think we are more virtuous, nor that others' frustrating idleness is, for some reason, deserved.

Hear our prayer in fervent hope that the day will come soon when all will have work and the dignity that it brings, and then joy of rest when work is done.

For the Incarcerated and Those Working in Prison

Tenacious and compassionate God, you who hold on to us when we have lost our way, be close to _____ today, whose days and nights are a routine of remembering choices that could have been better and of uneasiness about the future.

Facing the outcomes of what the penal system holds for *him/her,* knowing as well as the tentative assurances of a new start, bless _____, as *he/she* struggles with both the loneliness and the darkness of *his/her* days, with unconditional love and surprising grace.

For One in Military Service

In times of both war and peace men and women in military service live with the uncertainty of being called to active duty. Concern for their safety and separation from home and family is always close to the surface of everyone's thoughts and prayers.

Today we pray for _____, who knows the presence of enemy forces and the inner turmoil about life's uncertainties. Watch over _____ wherever *he/she* goes, letting love surround *him/her* in the midst of physical and emotional exhaustion, and may *he/she* know that family and church are spiritual partners with *him/her* for daily strength and courage.

Prayers for Ongoing Illness

For One Living with a Disability

When you, kind God, have reminded me that your "grace is sufficient for all my needs in Christ Jesus," I have been thankful that you have also given me confidence that I perhaps have gifts to give that others do not have.

Thank you for the possibility that in my comfort with my oneness with you, I can put others at ease who are uncomfortable with what they see in me as incomplete.

Praise to you for the wholeness I feel about myself in your great love for me.

For Learning Disorders

God of all knowledge, our society places so much value on what we know that we are misers of learning, stockpiling facts like treasured gold. _____ needs help to learn. We pray that you would heal and help *him/her* uncover the excitement of knowledge, the joy of reading, and the confidence of skills that currently frustrate *him/her*. However, remind us that it is not information that you prize, O God; heaven loves wisdom and those ranked last may well teach those who think they are head of the class.

Wise souls live simple, godly lives. If we accumulate every skill and memorize all the facts, we are still poor and ignorant if we do not know our God and cannot love like Jesus. Creator, you so often choose the ones who are most empty of worldly knowledge to be filled with treasures of heavenly wisdom. Help _____ to learn, value, and apply the lessons of Christ. And, as _____ learns of heaven's hope, help *him/her* to teach us.

Amen.

For One Dealing with Lingering Illness

God of enduring and patient love, _____

has been so ill for so long that we call it chronic, and for *him/her* the days and weeks are like a sentence on *his/her* hopes and courage. Hear _____ when *he/she* cries out in pain and broods about your attention to *his/her* despair, wondering how this could be a part of your intention for *his/her* life.

_____'s love for you is not in question nor does _____ doubt ultimately your healing grace, in whatever form it comes. So our prayer is for comfort, strength and reassurances that nothing can ever separate _____ from you.

For a Psychotic Patient

God of sympathy and tenderness, confident that your Spirit intercedes on behalf of those unable to muster what is needed for them to be engaged fully with mind and spirit, we pray for _____, who perhaps at present has little idea of how or what to pray.

May *he/she* know our love and care for *him/her* run deep. In *his/her* time of emotional pain and confusion, help *him/her* to be spared judgmental messages about *himself/herself* from within or without.

If *he/she* contemplates self-destructive solutions, sensing they would bring final relief, tell *him/her* through your Holy Spirit's power and intimacy that *he/she* is good and loved just as *he/she* is.

And let that same Spirit join all the forces of human compassion—professional counsel, right medication, heartfelt prayer—into one strong collaboration of comfort and peace for _____, all by the grace of the Lord Jesus Christ.

For One Suffering with Dementia or Alzheimer's Disease

How painful, God, to realize that _____ is becoming a different person right before our eyes. Knowing well that *he/she* is still our beloved one in the deep and beautiful places of the heart, *he/she* now presents *himself/herself* in ways foreign both to *him/her* and to us. Thank you for all the gifts of *his/her* life that we treasure in memory and in our sharing times with *him/her* in this new day. Help us as we grieve what seems lost and pray for grace and courage as we accustom our eyes and hearts to the changing scene.

For One Who Is Developmentally Disabled and Facing Medical Treatment

What unusual courage thrives in _____, who today is anticipating treatment again. *His/Her* life experience, profoundly different from mine, is nonetheless an inspiration by virtue of *his/her* incredible disposition, heart-opening and love-giving.

I pray today that this amazing collection of medical and technological equipment and sometimes strange procedures will not add to *his/her* anxiety, and that the personnel that form the healing team will reassure *him/her* with both calm understanding and healing peace.

Prayers for Healing

෨

A General Healing Prayer

Holy God, for many in our family, church and community, these are times of trial and uncertainty, anxiety and pain. There have been strains in relationships, recurrence of bad memories and disturbing dreams.

We pray today that by your healing grace the things in people's lives that seem to be tearing them apart will start yielding their control.

May they find that sharing their grief or disillusionment with trusted others will lighten the burden, that being yoked with you will find them carrying only half the weight and that each day they will discover your love again to such degree that the healing they receive is the healing you intend.

For Healing

Hear us, Holy One, as illness has come and with it the hope and prayer that its visit will be short-lived. Yet _____ experiences the reality that healing has not yet come, so we offer our prayers for *him/her* that if diagnosis is still uncertain, a recovery plan not yet in place, or progress with medication or other interventions not yet evident, _____ will still sense your participation with *him/her* and all these medical and spiritual resources so that soon _____ will be well again.

In the meantime, give *him/her* peace knowing you never leave us alone and desire our well-being even more than we do.

For Healing

Holy and gracious God, you with spotless record as listener, you whose spirit blows freely not only as teacher and comforter but as companion tireless, thanks be to you for enfleshing yourself in Jesus, who came alongside us and encourages us still to come alongside each other to share and help heal the diseases that find us and wear us out. And praise to you for this day reminding us we have a marvelous and life-giving stake in each other's lives and the lives of those who hunger and thirst for friendship and communion where there is evidence of spiritual promise and loving care.

Help us now to go gently into the world with arms that embrace, minds that cut through un-truth, hearts that capture large and small enemies by the strength of love as we are inheritors of the Spirit and brothers and sisters in Christ.

For Healing

We are bold to pray, healing God, for the sick, the hospitalized, those wounded by troubling dreams and old memories. Be present to those who await restoration and reassurances that pain is temporary. Thank you for the revelations that discomfort often brings—that we are given minds and bodies which, most of the time, function so dependably that we take your creative genius for granted. Be especially close to those family circles and friendships alerted to your healing graces by difficulties that have come to interrupt their sense of security.

And keep us aware always that our ultimate heal-ing is to be, in all things and conditions, right with you and in your healing presence.

Thanksgiving for Healing

Healing, redeeming Lord, in the midst of all our laments about how sick is our life, our culture, our environment, nevertheless you bring health and peace so that although our pains and unhappinesses here and there are chronic, deep in the canyon of our souls things are right. You are there and we are empowered.

Let the sick and troubled among us here, which means all of us, find and touch you. Thank you that the table is set with grace and that we eat and drink eagerly as those who have learned a long time ago where to find life in the midst of all our deaths. And as we reach, let us find that as we intrude on your larger story of your created world, we are named, loved and made bold to pray as we have been taught: "Our Father . . ."

Thanksgiving for Healing

Praise and thanksgiving, Lord, for the wonder of recovery, the journey toward full healing and for everything and everyone whose skills and prayers combined to ease the pain and close the wounds. We know that you, however, are the one who really heals.

As energy continues to return and confidence builds again, and relief is supremely what *I/we* feel more and more each day, hear *my/our* great thanksgiving for the peace you bring and the joy *I/we* celebrate.

For One Suffering with Depression

Just today, God, _____ has told me with palpable sadness that *he/she* is overcome with an emptiness that frightens *him/her* and that all of life seems bleak with a darkness unforgiving. _____ knows in *his/her* mind that you and *his/her* friends care deeply and that you, God, love *him/her* no matter what. But what _____ knows intellectually hasn't found residence in the core of *his/her* being just now.

Remind _____ today that the cycle of despair will be broken and light will return to *his/her* darkness, that _____ is held by grace even when *he/she* feels that nothing holds *him/her* steady or secure right now.

Bless us as we reach out to _____ with love and patient support, and bless those with the unique skills who help you heal with the Spirit's gifts of compassion and insight.

And let *him/her* know that shame and hurt, old or fresh, are covered by the wonder of your forgiveness.

For One Struggling with Addiction

Promising, faithful God, you who do not leave or forsake even when we are overcome with addictive forces and constant battles of the will, today _____ is in the midst of the struggle, and we pray that *he/she* will be unbound and set free. Let _____ know that you join *him/her* in the fray against whatever angers or fears or deep-seated pains fuel the temptations and desires that now hold *him/her* both bound and guilty.

Give _____ courage to find mutual support from those who understand and keep *him/her* accountable in participating with you in the healing that will surely come.

For One with HIV or AIDS

With courage and bravery _____ has drawn us into *his/her* confidence and soul by revealing *his/her* HIV/AIDS infection. *He/she* does not hide *his/her* fears and despair, *his/her* grief in the loss of friends and the abandonment of many who are quick to blame and judge.

Stay close when *he/she* has difficulty eating or sleeping and when *he/she* envisions a deteriorating future, even death itself, reminding *him/her* that even when *he/she* struggles with guilt, anger or shame, you are always, always love and that you will never leave or forsake *him/her.*

We pray for that healing that reassures that between _____ and you, your embrace signals everlasting love.

For One Facing Surgery

Gracious, comforting God, bless _____ today with the calm collectedness of one resting quietly in your strong yet tender care.

There is so much about surgery that could find us unsettled: the possibility of unexpected discoveries, the loss of control for minutes or hours, trust in surgeons' skills and costs of care. Help us to hand all these anxieties and fears over to you, knowing that you are not only consistently faithful when our lives run routinely, but also aware that you are especially near in life's emergencies.

So bless _____ now with an awareness that *he/she* is loved and held in the prayers of many who breathe *his/her* name today.

PRAYERS FOR A MARRIAGE

For Retrieving the Promises of Marriage

Patient God, hear our prayers for _____
and _____, who yearn for a return to the
days when marriage was fresh and more beautiful
than it is today for them. The years have brought
them through birth and death, creating and destroy-
ing, loyalty and betrayal, and now they long for the
joy of beginnings and of passion.

Grant them the new beginnings of forgiveness,
shared dreams and hopes, reconciliation where division hurts their mutual peace and the uncluttered
time together when they grew new as they grow
older. Let their reassurance that you still partner

with them in their promises, which they first made years ago, be a large part of their renewal.

For Bearing a Marriage Crisis

God, in whom all things are possible, help *me/ us/*_____ *and* _____ to face this marital crisis, believing that your Holy Spirit can restore the life to these dead days and feelings if *I am/ we are/they are* open to your counsel in the chambers of *my heart/our hearts/their hearts*.

Show *me/us/them* what cries out for forgiveness, teach *me/us/them* again the power of tenderness, and grant *me/us/them* new infusions of trust both in each other and in you, that *I/we/they* can find *my/our/their* marriage anchored again in grace and renewal.

For Those in the Midst of Divorce

Merciful God, _____ and _____, now divorced, are just beginning to come to grips with this deathlike experience. Search the dark rooms of their lives for the light of courage and peace to help them emerge from the anger and woundedness they are smothered with there.

Let each day find them losing the desire for revenge and the pain of battle, finding rather, by your grace, the journey of forgiveness and the recovery of worth and dignity.

For After Divorce, Moving or Changing Churches

Gracious God,
It is in remembering that I see your hand.
It is in remembering sadness that I see I was
        not alone
But was held by you,
In tears shared, in hands held in prayer

And I touched your hem . . .

In leaving, I learned of loss, but you did not
        let me lose you.

At times, when I felt I was losing my way,
        you called my name and drew me back
        with cords of love . . . a kind word, a
        call, a note.

And I touched your hem . . .

In the ending of a marriage you carried me
        through. You walked with me, giving
        me others who had made the journey
        before me, who shared their pain and

accompanied me. You taught me to be
free of resentment; you taught me how
to forgive.

And I touched your hem . . .

The darkness gradually became light, within
and without, reminding me of Peter's
words to "pay attention to you, to your
Word, as to a light shining in a dark place,
until the day dawns and the morning star
rises in my heart." You blessed me with a
new place, a new home.

And I touched your hem . . .

You provided. You did not leave me alone to
help children through their college
years. When I felt the challenges and
worries were too much to bear, you gave
me strength.

And I touched your hem . . .

You gave me courage in changing churches,
ever reminding me that I am a part of
the body of Christ in the world,
shaped by all who have gone before
me, who are with me now and who are
yet to come.

And I touched your hem . . .

May I look forward with trust, with discernment, not forgetting what is behind but
moving toward what lies ahead in the
name of Jesus Christ. My heart is
grateful, my spirit is willing, for I have
touched your hem. Amen.

Scripture

Love is patient; love is kind; love is not envious or
boastful or arrogant or rude. It does not insist on its
own way; it is not irritable or resentful; it does not
rejoice in wrongdoing, but rejoices in the truth. It
bears all things, believes all things, hopes all things,
endures all things.

Love never ends. But as for prophecies, they will
come to an end; as for tongues, they will cease; as for
knowledge, it will come to an end. For we know
only in part, and we prophesy only in part; but when
the complete comes, the partial will come to an end.
When I was a child, I spoke like a child, I thought
like a child, I reasoned like a child; when I became
an adult, I put an end to childish ways. For now we
see in a mirror, dimly, but then we will see face to
face. Now I know only in part; then I will know fully,

even as I have been fully known. And now faith, hope, and love abide, these three; and the greatest of these is love. (1 Corinthians 13:4-13 NRSV)

Love never gives up.
Love cares more for others than for self.
Love doesn't want what it doesn't have.
Love doesn't strut,
Doesn't have a swelled head,
Doesn't force itself on others,
Isn't always "me first,"
Doesn't fly off the handle,
Doesn't keep score of the sins of others,
Doesn't revel when others grovel,
Takes pleasure in the flowering of truth,
Puts up with anything,
Trusts God always,
Always looks for the best,
Never looks back,
But keeps going to the end.

Love never dies. Inspired speech will be over some day; praying in tongues will end; understanding will reach its limit. We know only a portion of the truth, and what we say about God is always incomplete. But when the Complete arrives, our incompletes will be canceled.

When I was an infant at my mother's breast, I gurgled and cooed like any infant. When I grew up, I left those infant ways for good.

We don't yet see things clearly. We're squinting in a fog, peering through a mist. But it won't be long before the weather clears and the sun shines bright! We'll see it all then, see it all as clearly as God sees us, knowing him directly just as he knows us!

But for right now, until that completeness, we have three things to do to lead us toward that consummation: Trust steadily in God, hope unswervingly, love extravagantly. And the best of the three is love. (1 Corinthians 13:4-13 *The Message*)

There is no fear in love, but perfect love casts out fear; for fear has to do with punishment, and whoever fears has not reached perfection in love. (1 John 4:18 NRSV)

There is no room in love for fear. Well-formed love banishes fear. Since fear is crippling, a fearful life—fear of death, fear of judgment—is one not yet fully formed in love. (1 John 4:18 *The Message*)

PRAYERS FOR PARENTS AND CHILDREN

For Parents with a Pregnancy at Risk

Gracious God, always alert when our cries for help seem more urgent than usual, we are anxious for a baby yet unborn. This child of _____ and _____ is at risk of being lost during pregnancy, and we are bold to pray that the baby will survive this critical time.

Hold _____ and _____, as waiting is difficult and hope needs refueling, sleep is restless and faith binds them to you and to each other.

A Husband's Prayer for His Wife During Childbirth

Mighty and tender God, be close now, very close to

_____, my loving and faithful wife, and let both fear and pain be defended by your faithful hold on her life.

When our child is taken carefully and tenderly from her, may her joy and mine grant her a kind of divine forgetfulness of the momentary ordeal. I offer praise and thanksgiving for our child on the way. Give him or her the full breath of life, good health for body, mind and soul, and help us never to forget the miracle.

For a Child Born with Physical Challenges

Faithful, dependable God, hear our prayers as we try to absorb this painful surprise in the lives of _____ and _____ today. Upon waking to anticipate and celebrate the arrival of precious __[name of child]__, their prayers of thanksgiving for new life are tempered with prayers for bravery as they face new and unknown challenges raising _____ who, newly born, carries special needs.

As they confess their honest fears, allow them as well to find and nourish this blessing now gifting their lives, above all knowing you are with them all the time and that by your grace all the varied experiences of their life now will draw them ever closer to each other and to you.

For Parents Adopting a Child

Surprising, faithful God, the intense and prayerful negotiations between agencies, friends and your generous Holy Spirit have given _____ and _____ the blessed gift of a child who has opened their hearts, changed their lives profoundly and confirmed for them your ultimate care.

Remind _____ and _____ that you have an abiding delivery of adoptive grace by adopting us all into your holy family as cherished children. And show this child, _____, throughout *his/her* life that *his/her* adoption into this excited family is clear evidence that the Holy Spirit does wondrous, life-giving things.

For Parents Placing a Child for Adoption

Loving, faithful God, _ _____'s decision to offer up this child for adoption touches the deep places of our hearts. We are grateful for the healthy birthtime of child and mother, thankful as well that in your love and wisdom you have given strength and courage to face the wide range of emotions during pregnancy and giving birth. The marvel of feeling life within and the sorrows felt anticipating this day of separation are profoundly mixed. From this day forward, may *they/he/she* be at peace, comforted by your reassurances and tender care, at ease with the trust *they/he/she have/has* in you.

Bless the new home with all your best gifts for these loving parents and tender child. Grant them such spiritual nurture as to sustain them in all things.

For a Child in Shared Custody

Loving and watchful God, bless _____, that as *he/she* lives now in what could be an insecure world were it not for your promise of companionship and love, *he/she* will also know that *he/she* is not far away from the hearts of both mother and father. Let _____ be spared undue anxiety about *his/her* parents' difficult relationship with each other, so that when present with each from time to time, _____ will be blessed with love's joy and keenly aware of being bonded in love with each and with you.

For a Struggling Adolescent

Here we are tonight, Lord, with you and
_____, whose unhappiness, even despair, arises in a body that is shattered and a heart torn to pieces. We, with *him/her*, sometimes lose confidence that there is precious hope in the night. Many have already condemned and others avoid *him/her*, anxious to avoid contagion.

Help _____ to know that deep in your heart and ours *he/she* is longed for and loved, that you, faithful companion to the prodigal, are eager and able to breathe new life and speak again and again the good news of redemption, that nothing is lost but all can be restored.

For Young People When the Pressure Is On

Today, Holy God, _____ seems to be uptight about something or other. We have learned that young people today juggle much on their journey. We wish we could just grant them a good day at the beach or in the park with a fun book for a change and blot out everything that has them anxious most of the time.

Competition for grades, popularity, stardom on

stage or on the field would be enough, but there is also for pressure from teachers, TV and parents as well as technological overload.

Bless _____ today. Open the pressure valves. Let _____ know *he/she* is loved unconditionally by you and us. And show us ways in which we may be part of the easing-up and not part of the grip.

For Those Caring for Aging Parents

God, your presence so needed when worries about our aging parents occupy our nights and days, be close to __[names of caregivers]__, who know the constant anxiety and fear for what the future holds.

May the strong and sustaining memories of their own childhoods, where they trusted fully in their parents, now reward them with the thought of returning the favor. Help them to be good listeners, to speak truth when called for, to accept the wear and tear of long hours' demands, and to bear the emotional rigors knowing that the love by which these gifts are offered to *mother/father* are gifts of yours to them as well.

Prayers for Celebrations

For a Wedding Celebration

Faithful God, today _____ and
_____ will find many reasons to celebrate the good life together, sensing how kind and
gracious you have been.

The memories shared will be washed with tears
of both joy and sadness, from bright days unusu-
ally happy to those clouded with gray difficulty. All
are packaged today in a satisfying bundle, and they
know that you will be along for the journey as
great companion.

May their dominant recollections be those of
your benediction, deep and honest, on their com-

mitment to reaching beyond themselves to others with warmth, encouragement and open hearts. And let them have a sense of vision for many years of the same.

Thanksgiving for Age

This getting old, God, accompanies the journey with ever-growing symptoms unmistakable. Good things just take more time, and infirmities large or small remind me that I was so very fortunate for so many years to be healthy and fortified, making my life both joy and miracle.

So as I move more slowly, perhaps remember fewer things that happened even recently, and my body complains of wear and tear, keep giving me a spirit of gratitude and gifts of love and good humor to pass along to others who may not know how good you are through the changes and accidents of time.

For One Who Has Survived Abuse

God of freedom, the scratches etched on the record of my soul from loss of security, dignity and serenity in the prison of abuse's power are losing their sting with me, and I am praising your name and power for the liberation of healing grace.

Knowing the indelible marks of painful memory will linger, your Spirit-wind has rustled my faith coals with warmth and, among many wonderful things, I feel safe again.

Every day I am more conscious of the healing than the wounds, for which my soul rejoices.

Completion of a Habitat for Humanity Home

Great, joyful God, on this warm and sun-drenched day, we come with smiles and tears and with hearts beating faster and louder. For some here have lived all their lives without seeing a miracle, and some never realized they could be partners with you in one. Today we stand in awe that what was once here rubble and mud is the evidence of dreams come true.

Thank you, kind Lord, for allowing us the joy of joining hearts and hands with these courageous families who now call this home. For those who gave the most of body strength and soul support, we acknowledge what a fulfilling moment this must truly be. Let them not be ashamed to feel the satisfaction of worthy work and the sound of your voice today saying, "Good job, good job."

Bless with special grace these our friends who now call this home. Let the days grow richer for them with their new responsibilities as homeowners, their nights filled with the rest that comes from knowing that hope does thrive again and that brothers and sisters in the faith are praying for them in the future that has more promise than before.

Teach us all something today, O Master Builder. Build us up where we are torn down. Hide us a while with you, so that seeing straight and nourished by your life and Spirit we will feel all the more like walking your way and doing your will.

In the name and power of Christ our Lord, who brings to these ceremonies the deep and abiding joy that makes this celebration.

On Being Released from Prison

I have left the iron bars and the big gate today, Lord. My feet shake and my heartbeat races. Fresh air seems like luxury because it flows everywhere.

As I rejoice, I recognize that I will keep promises, clarify and make good choices, and lead a productive life only with the support of family, friends and spiritual renewal day by day.

Keep me strong in recovery and transition; encourage those who still love me to support and enable my new life. Alert me to the wondrous truth that nothing is lost, that redemption means even the tough times of our past are caught up, turned in, covered over by your grace.

Prayers for Home and Church

At Church Before Worship

Holy God, full of grace and just in all your ways, come to church with us this day with the urgency of your call to faith and the wonder of your large and magnificent promises.

For so many in our times there are long stretches when the good news is stale news.

For some there are times when they are unable to vouch for the gospel with the joy it deserves, caught in the abundance of life's chores. Spare us when so much distracts us. Spare us the corrosion of our enthusiasms, the impurity of our purposes and the deterioration of our courage. For if you do not enter our lives day after day, we may miss our charge to reach out to that segment of humanity that continues to stumble for unrighteousness's sake.

Say something today, God, by peace or persuasion, assurance or confirmation, as we anticipate by singing, listening, praying you're meeting us here with differing hopes and wounds.

A General Prayer, Especially on Sunday

Loving Lord of heaven and earth, you have given us this day. It is a given yet an unusual gift. What this day offers in the corners and flat places of the world gives it a different twist—from hot tenement where life is cursed to deep green valley where folks fear no evil—you are with your world. All is in your hands. The day is given. Christ is risen! Praise be to you again.

We seek mercy to be healed again. We come crippled by bad choices and by unfortunate and sinful deeds, and by failure to do anything really redemptive when we know we had the chance. But you are the healer, the forgiver. So we are bold enough to believe that you have already forgotten what we did or didn't do—that you have closed the door on all of that. Now let repentance really mean something by our resolve that we sin like that no more!

Hear our joy and our sorrows. Listen to our needs. Walk with those we name in intercession. And bless your Word upon our lives. Give it more than a narrow channel guarded closely by our own persuasions.

In the freedom of your Spirit's love.

For Sitting Ready in Church, Waiting for Worship to Unfold

Only you know, Lord, what is in the hearts of all of us who have said "yes" this morning to your call to worship.

We seem to hear the unstifled sighs of those who are just happy to sit for an hour and rest; the week has been that demanding and that much of a strain. We know that is all right with you, for you ask us to come for rest and for the unshouldering of our burdens.

For some there is a new appreciation for life because you have restored their joy or their peace of mind.

For others there is the hope that today will be the day when the darkness rolls up on one side and the light stands shining on the other, and they can say how good it is to be alive. May this be a day of spiritual daybreak for all of us.

Grant world leadership wisdom to figure out how to stop bloodshed and threatening speech, how to give courage and new hope to oppressed peoples, how to find spiritual plenty for the world's spiritual hunger, so that one day we may all raise a great chorus of joy.

Traditional Table Graces

Be Present at Our Table, Lord
Be present at our table, Lord;
Be here and everywhere adored.
These mercies bless, and grant that we
May feast in fellowship with thee.

God Is Great
God is great, and God is good,
And we thank him for our food;
By his hand we all are fed;
Give us, Lord, our daily bread.

For Health and Strength and Daily Food
For health and strength and daily food,
We praise thy name, O Lord.

God, We Thank You for This Food

God, we thank you for this food.

For rest and home and all things good.

For wind and rain and sun above.

But most of all for those we love.

Give Us Grateful Hearts, Our Father

Give us grateful hearts, our Father,

for all your mercies,

and make us mindful of the needs of others;

through Christ our Lord.

Dear Lord, Thank You for the Gift of Food

Dear Lord, thank you for the gift of food

You've placed upon our table.

And help us all to do your work

In any way we're able.

We Thank Thee, Lord, for Happy Hearts

We thank thee, Lord, for happy hearts,

For rain and sunny weather.

We thank thee, Lord, for this food,

And that today we are together.

Bless These Your Gifts, Most Gracious God

Bless these your gifts, most gracious God,

From whom all goodness springs;

Make clean our hearts and feed our souls

With good and joyful things.

To God Who Gives Us Daily Bread

To God who gives us daily bread

A thankful song we raise,

And pray that he who sends us food

Will fill our hearts with praise.

A Liturgy for the Blessing of a Home

*All may gather at the door. The leader may dip an
evergreen branch into a bowl of water and sprinkle water
on the door and on those gathered as he or she says:*

Leader 1: Peace be to this house and to all who
enter it!

—paraphrased from Luke 10:5

All: **Amen.**

Leader 2: Unless the Lord builds the house,

All: **those who build it labor in vain.**

—Psalm 127:1

The door is opened and all gather inside the door.

Leader 1: Jesus said,
"Those who love me will keep my word,
and my Father will love them,
and we will come to them and make
our home with them."

—John 14:23, adapt.

Householder: As for me and my household, we
               will serve the Lord.

—Joshua 24:15

All: **Thanks be to God.**

A candle may be lighted and presented to a member of the household.

Leader 1:   This is the message we have heard
            from God and proclaim to you,
            that God is light and in God there is
            no darkness at all.

—1 John 1:5, adapt.

Leader 2:   Let us pray.
            O God of light, continue to shed your
            light throughout this home,
            that all who live here and all who
            find hospitality here
            may dwell in the radiance of your
            presence;
            through Jesus Christ,
            the Light of the world.

All: **Amen.**

The assembly moves to a living room or family room.

Leader 1:   Jesus said,
            "Where two or three are gathered
            in my name,
            there am I in the midst of them."

—Matthew 18:20, RSV

*A cross or house blessing certificate may be placed
on the wall.*

Leader 2: Let us pray.
Lord Jesus, be present in this household,
not only as the holy guest but also as
the extravagant host,
welcoming all who gather here,
without distinction,
into the warm embrace of your
reconciling and redeeming love,

All: **Amen.**

The assembly moves to the kitchen or dining room.

Leader 1: All your works shall give thanks to
you, O Lord,

All: **and all your faithful shall bless you.**

Leader 1: The eyes of all look to you,
and you give them their food in due
season.

All: **You open your hand, satisfying the desire
of every living thing.**

—Psalm 145:10, 15-16, adapt.

Leader 2: You fill your people, O God, with
good things—
good things to feed and nourish the
body,
good things to satisfy the longing of
the soul.
Bless those who prepare food
and bless those who eat it,
that, as Jesus on the day of resurrection

broke bread with two disciples, all
who gather here
may have their eyes opened and
recognize him
as a holy presence at this table.

All: **Amen.**

The assembly may move to a bedroom.

Leader 1: Let the light of your face shine on us,
O Lord!

All: **You have put gladness in my heart, more
than when grain and wine abound.**

Leader 1: I will both lie down and sleep in peace;

All: **for you alone, O Lord, make me lie down
in safety.**

—*Psalm 4:6-8*

Leader 2: Sanctify, O God, our lying down
and our rising up,
that, whether asleep or awake,
we may be kept in your care
and always refreshed by
your renewing grace.

All: **Amen.**

*After this final prayer, assembly will return to the kitchen
for refreshments and a final prayer of thanksgiving.*

Leader 1: Jesus said,

"Abide in me as I abide in you.
Just as the branch cannot bear fruit by
itself

unless it abides in the vine,
neither can you unless you abide in me.
I am the vine, you are the branches.
Those who abide in me and I in them
bear much fruit,
because apart from me you can do
nothing."

—*John 15:4-5*

Leader 2: Let us pray.
Bless this house, O God,
and sanctify those who dwell here,
that this may be a home for you,
a dwelling place for your abiding.

All: **Amen.**

Leader 1: *Addressing the members of the household:*

The Lord is your keeper;
The Lord will keep your life.
The Lord will keep your going out
and your coming in
from this time on and forevermore.

—*Psalm 121:5, 7, 8, adapt.*

Leader 1: *Addressing all:*

The peace of the Lord Jesus Christ be
with you.

All: **And also with you.**

The assembly may exchange expressions of peace.

Praying for Our Larger World

Environment

Loving God, we give thanks that your world is our home. You have decorated it with canyons and cascades, open oceans and intricate inlets, broad deserts and deep rainforests, mountains and plains. The beauty of our home is wondrous to behold. You have stocked it with plentiful resources of food and water, materials for construction, and areas for recreation. The bounty that surrounds us in our home amazes us. You have filled it with companions of all sorts, furred and feathered, scaled and shelled, species upon species. The blend of inhabitants within our home enriches us.

Forgive us, we pray, for the poor care we give to the home you provide us. We have made alterations that destroy the work of your hands and that weaken the good earth's structure and balance. We have wasted supplies, spoiled our living space, and acted with irresponsibility as tenants of your world. We have consumed without conscience as if our greed had no consequences for our neighbors.

Grant us a renewed appreciation for our home, and charge us with the reverence and responsibility to keep it well. In the name of Jesus Christ, creation's Ruler.

Amen.

Elections

Creator and Sustainer of the world, hear our prayers for national and world leaders and for those who have access to their minds and ears, who advise and counsel, that together with all those who carry both the vigor and sensitivity of common people far removed from political games, the honor and decency of mutual peace and respect might flourish everywhere.

Global Issues

Listening and revealing God, let us be conscious always of your spirit nudging us to reflect upon, and respond to, national and international issues, moral choices, political leadership, so that our list of sins does not include preoccupation with self to the exclusion of what we can do and be as your living body in the earth.

Thank you for counting us your partners joined with you in ordering a livable world, with enduring evidences of your gifts of reconciliation and redemption.

Justice

You shall not pervert the justice due to your poor in their lawsuits. Keep far from a false charge, and do not kill the innocent and those in the right, for I will not acquit the guilty. You shall take no bribe, for a bribe blinds the officials, and subverts the cause of those who are in the right.

You shall not oppress a resident alien; you know the heart of an alien, for you were aliens in the land of Egypt. (Exodus 23:6-9 NRSV)

When there is a dispute concerning your poor, don't tamper with the justice due them.

Stay clear of false accusations. Don't contribute to the death of innocent and good people. I don't let the wicked off the hook.

Don't take bribes. Bribes blind perfectly good eyes and twist the speech of good people.

Don't take advantage of a stranger. You know what it's like to be a stranger; you were strangers in Egypt. (Exodus 23:6-9 *The Message*)

> Cease to do evil,
> learn to do good;
> seek justice,
> rescue the oppressed,
> defend the orphan,
> plead for the widow. (Isaiah 1:16-17 NRSV)

> Say no to wrong.
> Learn to do good.
> Work for justice.
> Help the down-and-out.
> Stand up for the homeless.
> Go to bat for the defenseless.
>   (Isaiah 1:16-17 *The Message*)

Ah, you who make iniquitous decrees,
who write oppressive statutes,
to turn aside the needy from justice
and to rob the poor of my people of their right,

that widows may be your spoil,
and that you may make the orphans your
        prey! (Isaiah 10:1-2 NRSV)

Doom to you who legislate evil, who make
        laws that make victims—Laws that
        make misery for the poor,
    that rob my destitute people of dignity,
Exploiting defenseless widows,
    taking advantage of homeless children.
        (Isaiah 10:1-2 *The Message*)

Is not this the fast that I choose:
        to loose the bonds of injustice,
        to undo the thongs of the yoke,
to let the oppressed go free,
and to break every yoke?
Is it not to share your bread with the hungry,
        and bring the homeless poor into your
        house;
when you see the naked, to cover them,
        and not to hide yourself from your own
        kin?
Then your light shall break forth like the
        dawn,
        and your healing shall spring up
        quickly;
your vindicator shall go before you,

the glory of the LORD shall be your rear
guard.
Then you shall call, and the LORD will answer;
you shall cry for help, and he will say,
Here I am.

If you remove the yoke from among you,
the pointing of the finger, the speaking
of evil,
if you offer your food to the hungry
and satisfy the needs of the afflicted,
then your light shall rise in the darkness
and your gloom be like the noonday.
The LORD will guide you continually,
and satisfy your needs in parched
places,
and make your bones strong;
and you shall be like a watered garden,
like a spring of water,
whose waters never fail.
(Isaiah 58:6-11 NRSV)

This is the kind of fast day I'm after:
to break the chains of injustice,
get rid of exploitation in the workplace,
free the oppressed,
cancel debts.
What I'm interested in seeing you do is:

sharing your food with the hungry,
inviting the homeless poor into your
homes,
putting clothes on the shivering ill-clad,
being available to your own families.
Do this and the lights will turn on,
and your lives will turn around at once.
Your righteousness will pave your way.
The God of glory will secure your passage.
Then when you pray, God will answer.
You'll call out for help and I'll say, 'Here
I am.'

If you get rid of unfair practices,
quit blaming victims,
quit gossiping about other people's sins,
If you are generous with the hungry
and start giving yourselves to the
down-and-out,
Your lives will begin to glow in the darkness,
your shadowed lives will be bathed in
sunlight.
I will always show you where to go.
I'll give you a full life in the emptiest of
places—firm muscles, strong bones.
You'll be like a well-watered garden,
a gurgling spring that never runs dry.
(Isaiah 58:6-11 *The Message*)

Seek good and not evil,
> that you may live;
and so the LORD, the God of hosts, will be
> with you,
> > just as you have said.
Hate evil and love good,
> and establish justice in the gate;
it may be that the LORD, the God of hosts,
> will be gracious to the remnant of
> Joseph. . . .
But let justice roll down like waters,
> and righteousness like an everflowing
> stream. (Amos 5:14-15, 24 NRSV)

Seek good and not evil—
> and live!
You talk about God, the God-of-the-Angel-
> Armies,
> being your best friend.
Well, live like it,
> and maybe it will happen.

Hate evil and love good,
> then work it out in the public square.
Maybe God, the God-of-the-Angel-Armies,
> will notice your remnant and be
> gracious. . . .
Do you know what I want?

I want justice—oceans of it.
I want fairness—rivers of it.
    That's what I want. That's all I want.
    (Amos 5:14-15, 24 *The Message*)

We know love by this, that he laid down his life for us—and we ought to lay down our lives for one another. How does God's love abide in anyone who has the world's goods and sees a brother or sister in need and yet refuses help?

Little children, let us love, not in word or speech, but in truth and action. (1 John 3:16-18 NRSV)

This is how we've come to understand and experience love: Christ sacrificed his life for us. This is why we ought to live sacrificially for our fellow believers, and not just be out for ourselves. If you see some brother or sister in need and have the means to do something about it but turn a cold shoulder and do nothing, what happens to God's love? It disappears. And you made it disappear.

My dear children, let's not just talk about love; let's practice real love. (1 John 3:16-18 *The Message*)

God of freedom and liberty, keep granting to us more and more clarity about how to conduct ourselves in the face of broken agreements, ignored treaties, disregard for equal liberties. As the lights go out for freedom in many places of the world, paint a clear canvas for us, O God, that shows us in bright colors and clear lines when and where we need to fight, when and where to stop fighting, where to be tough is to be holy, where to pull out, where and when to give of our abundance in time so starving people of the world will not buy a bowl of soup and sell their liberty to get it. But help us not to blame them if they do, as we have often been unwilling Samaritans and barn-builders when our souls have been required.

O God, show us the authentic prophets of your Word for our time and let us hear your Word gladly.

Peace

Except a corn of wheat fall into the ground . . . (John 12:24)

For to this end Christ died and lived again, so that he might be Lord of both the dead and the living.

Why do you pass judgment on your brother or sister? Or you, why do you despise your brother or sister? For we will all stand before the judgment seat of God. For it is written,

"As I live, says the Lord, every knee shall bow
to me,
and every tongue shall give praise to God."

So then, each of us will be accountable to God.
Let us therefore no longer pass judgment on one another, but resolve instead never to put a stumbling
block or hindrance in the way of another. I know
and am persuaded in the Lord Jesus that nothing is
unclean in itself; but it is unclean for anyone who
thinks it unclean. (Romans 14:9-14 NRSV)

That's why Jesus lived and died and then lived
again: so that he could be our Master across the en-
tire range of life and death, and free us from the petty
tyrannies of each other.

So where does that leave you when you criticize
a brother? And where does that leave you when
you condescend to a sister? I'd say it leaves you
looking pretty silly—or worse. Eventually, we're
all going to end up kneeling side by side in the
place of judgment, facing God. Your critical and
condescending ways aren't going to improve your
position there one bit. Read it for yourself in
Scripture:

"As I live and breathe," God says,
"every knee will bow before me;
Every tongue will tell the honest truth
that I and only I am God."

So tend to your knitting. You've got your hands full just taking care of your own life before God.

Forget about deciding what's right for each other. Here's what you need to be concerned about: that you don't get in the way of someone else, making life more difficult than it already is. I'm convinced—Jesus convinced me!—that everything as it is in itself is holy. We, of course, by the way we treat it or talk about it, can contaminate it. (Romans 14:9-14 *The Message*)

Do not repay evil for evil or abuse for abuse; but, on the contrary, repay with a blessing. It is for this that you were called—that you might inherit a blessing. For

"Those who desire life
and desire to see good days,
let them keep their tongues from evil
and their lips from speaking deceit;
let them turn away from evil and do good;
let them seek peace and pursue it.

For the eyes of the Lord are on the righteous,
 and his ears are open to their prayer.
But the face of the Lord is against those who
 do evil."

Now who will harm you if you are eager to do
what is good? But even if you do suffer for doing
what is right, you are blessed. Do not fear what they
fear, and do not be intimidated, (1 Peter 3:9-14 NRSV)

No retaliation. No sharp-tongued sarcasm. Instead, bless—that's your job, to bless. You'll be a
blessing and also get a blessing.

Whoever wants to embrace life
 and see the day fill up with good,
Here's what you do:
 Say nothing evil or hurtful;
Snub evil and cultivate good;
 run after peace for all you're worth.
God looks on all this with approval,
 listening and responding well to what
 he's asked;
But he turns his back
 on those who do evil things.

If with heart and soul you're doing good, do you
think you can be stopped? Even if you suffer for it,

you're still better off. Don't give the opposition a second thought. (1 Peter 3:9-14 *The Message*)

> Before the crust of earth is
>> punctured by the first fragile
>> spear of grain hungry for the sun,
>> a signal sent from Sovereign
>> readies the world for full-blown harvest.

> Now hearts of steel are
>> bent by the growing warm
>> nudges of desire daring to be free;
>> the fire stoked by the Spirit
>> bursts the borders of aging differences.

> Ever the love of God is
>> moved by his first compassion,
>> impulses of peace seeking for a womb;
>> courage is nursed by his infant Son
>> renewing hope in these pregnant times.

Nation

Sovereign Lord, come to all our occasions of prayer and praise for our country. Thanks to you when we sense we are one people bound together and to you by trust nourished in great dreams and fundamental integrity.

But keep our celebrations honest as we think about the sacrifice endured for our sacred passions in times past, compassionate while we navigate the tense negotiations of the present, and confident that you will continue to be our cherished partner looking to a bright future.

And in the recognition of the reality of the world's penchant for hostility, give us always the strong resolve to be first to offer the alternative of peace, for ourselves and upon those who have wronged us and upon those whom we have wronged. Grant us your peace before the momentum of hatred overruns our capacity to control it.

Make us a servant people, following the way of our Lord Jesus Christ.

Praying for the Year's Seasons

General Prayer for All Seasons

Open us up, Lord, by the tender care of your Spirit, in our personal inward "houses." If our assurance from you is an eternal home in that wondrous place of many rooms, remind us today to visit the "rooms" of our own lives, which sometimes we have been afraid to visit.

There is the storage space where memories live, and some of those memories are neglected because of their pain. We have been afraid to touch because they are like tombs where we have temporarily given up or left things wrapped in a kind of death.

Perhaps there are banquet halls there that have not seen a good, hearty celebration—maybe even a small chapel that would come to life were there more visits for both praise and thanksgiving.

Thank you for always wanting to join us in all our "rooms" because you love us through and through. And that companionship will make the journey to your mansions, O God, seem like an easy step over the threshold.

General Prayer for All Seasons

Almighty God, we know the world is yours, this wide-horizoned, both sunny and cloud-covered, wind-dusted and mostly green world. Seeing your glory everywhere from hills to valleys and forests guarding our swift rivers, we remember to marvel.

Not always! Some of us are tense and restless, and the human drain of illness old and new, fleeting peace of mind and occasional deep doubts are just reminders that when we hurt, the cry of "O, that I knew where I might find him" leaps from a hiding place in our memory.

In all times of wonder and wound, thank you, God, that you stand behind the words "The Lord is the strength of my life; of whom (or what) shall I be afraid?" Grant us the assurance that today's blandness or heavy weight will yield again to the brightness and the glory of your dependable promises to stand next to us in all our needs and dreams.

And let your peace, love, power, compassion and Spirit come to life in those people who walk through our prayers right now and for whom we intercede for whatever causes them to yearn for something that might bring joy and healing into their lives.

General Prayer for All Seasons

Praise to you, God, with thanksgiving running deep that you do not forget us or forget our names. Our daily nourishment of grace and sure provisions remind us that great and mighty though you be, your gifts to us are often silently rich as mustard seed.

Thank you, God, thank you, and praise to you that you told us who love you to search and find and share with neighborhood and world citizens who long to live our dance of joy. You know their names, too. They are the frantic ones looking everywhere for freedom, dignity, good food, loyal friends, a place to settle and call home. Help us see even the despised ones and accept them, even as we have been accepted.

Help us to know the magnitude of your love and influence resting within us. And then confident that the power is yours, remind us that we have it not that our will but that your will may be done on earth as it is in heaven.

We Give Thanks for an Ordinary Day

We give thanks for water, refreshing,
cleansing,
And pray for those who have no
running water.

We give thanks for electricity, to make our
morning tea and coffee,
for the refrigerator, the hairdryer,
And pray for the coffee farmers, for fair trade,
for those with no electricity.

As we drop trash into the bin and
go to the dumpster,
We pray for those who seek food in dump-
sters,
or hide in them to keep warm.

As we give our pets water and food,
we delight in their presence
And pray for animals who are neglected,
whose habitat is being destroyed.

As we inhale the beauty of the
morning mountains and trees,
We pray for the places of deforestation
and give thanks for Wangari
Maathai, tree-planter, Nobel Peace Prize
winner.

As we get in our cars, we give
thanks for transportation,
And pray for those who walk,
for injustices in our world created around oil.
As we drive to work, we give thanks
that we have work,
And pray for the unemployed.

We take the call from the doctor's office,
telling us the test was just fine,
And pray for those whose results are not just
fine, and those who have no
access to medical care, or no health
insurance.

We give thanks for friends who visit,
sharing a simple meal,
And pray for the friendless and
those who always eat alone.

As we go to bed, we give thanks for rest,
for a place called home,

And we pray for those who live in shelters,
whose homes are destroyed
by war and violence.

And we give thanks for another Ordinary Day.

Spring

So much joy greets us at our spring windows, Lord. The blue and yellow embroidery of young flowers across the floor of your earth. The smell of just enough dew on young grass to make us eager to put the seeds down and watch the renewal of your world.

It is the time of year when it is not hard to think of the future. There is the planning that happens naturally—another coat of paint for the garage, filling the birdhouse with fresh seed, washing winter grunge from the windows.

We all come welcoming a springtime of the spirit. It is the season of resurrection, to move from war to peace, from imprisonment to freedom, from hunger for more to finding a full life. In Christ risen we can sing again in our sorrow, see possibilities for love to overcome strife; all people can experience the amazing gift of a clean break from sin and a run after the peace and joy of the Savior.

In the spring of our joy, give us drums and trumpets and help us let the world know redemption's music.

Summer

For this time of year when sun rests high and days stand still, praise to you, O God, for whatever of re-creation happens for us and for your beautiful world.

Our children play games on chalked sidewalks, and neighbors love their porches for sitting and sipping cool drinks, and we all rejoice that trees are full green and birds and bugs make noises that create a very fine chorus.

Keep making us attentive to good things and even good news, that large and small occasions on long days and evenings might keep us aware that you visit us these months with growing and nurturing surprises for us to enjoy at the time. Let us file them away too for times when news is bleak and gray days make us feel that life is flat and you seem far away.

In our best hours we are sure of your changeless love, and summer is the pledge of the brightest weather of the heart.

After Summer

Cold and damp we came this morning, just getting our first sample of autumn in our neighborhood. Now we have been warmed by summer memories, child-friendly and family-binding. Before red leaves fall and frost quickens our pace, praise to you for remembrances and thanksgivings. In your flourishing summer world you touched the youngest with new wonders of your Spirit in new friends and brave new discoveries of the love of Jesus; in the gathering of youth by the thousands, how wide and deep did they find your mercy and challenge to be; families, sometimes pulled in by the city's fragmenting demands and temptations, reconnected and grew stronger in the intimacy of days designed just for realizing how deliberately you yearn for their binding and their spiritual health. You blessed the mission trips with the wonder of lives hungry and lives transformed. Thanks be to you, O God, for all the witness we have heard to warm this chilly day.

Autumn

Holy God, these days we walk by the rich light of sun's bright glow at evening, being chased toward the other side of the world but gifting us in the meantime with long shadows and thanksgiving for good harvests.

Even the baskets on the field and in the stands by the country roads hold foods that last—hard-crusted squash, gourds that survive stubbornly.

Praise to you, Lord, for a time when reflection yields good memories of another good year, seed time and harvest and life laid down honestly in hard work and deliberate stewardship of breath and spirit. Above all, gratitude for life itself, sustained, loved and guarded by your faithfulness, stronger than our stubborn wills, more lasting than any temporary joys that endure only for a season.

As bright leaves fall and we begin to prepare to defend ourselves for shorter days under the sun, thanks for coming inside with us, filling us, as you always do, with your light and truth, and your own bright Holy Spirit.

Winter

With so much cold and rowdy wind it is sometimes easy to forget, kind Lord, that this is the season when you announced it is time to get ready for music and dancing on the white landscape of forgiveness, freedom and your own presence at heart and hearth.

Outside the occasional blizzard brings with it broken limbs and groaning trees, frozen ponds and long coats rescued from the back of the closet. All of it both enjoyed and endured, knowing that darkness yields one day to light and we can wait.

And like the impatience for that relief, we long for Jesus and God's great human touch, knowing that in him we will receive rescue where we cannot help ourselves, health we cannot heal and the life to which we cannot give birth.

Praise to you for Immanuel, God with us, who came just in the time of the earth's winter of the soul.

Winter into Spring

God of love's eternal flavor and joy, sometimes when we observe the reluctance of one season to yield to the next, we see a parallel in our own behaviors. Often we feel like winter hangs on too long for spring to come full bore, and rainy spells hang around or heat waves keep exhausting our energy. When the sun rises and the frozen ponds yield, we remember the faithfulness of the cycles that are both dependable and challenging.

At our best moments we live in hope that our hearts will flourish green like spring and that we will remember the times when you, O Lord, came at the right time and freshened the weather of our lives.

We saw you when the unexpected came our way and you stepped in to give strength where we were reluctant; we saw you when we wanted to say a word of power and reconciliation where nerves were raw and feelings between persons were ragged and abrasive, and you jogged our minds and moved our lips and somehow used us to help someone else; we saw you when we were unnecessarily harsh with our children and impatient with our mothers and fathers, and you made room in our hearts to live and love and overcome our sour dispositions; we saw you when we were so anxious about our health, or doubtful that tomorrow would bring a better shake, and you softened the blow and reminded us of our little faith.

Keep in touch, Lord, keep in touch, showing us how you keep us growing in all the seasons of our lives.

A Morning Prayer

Our Father, who are in heaven,

—long time ago, now, when dark and light were still not separated, you stepped out and made a world, beautiful and bold and sometimes fearful, a first birth of wonder and surprise.

Holy is your name

—powerful enough for six days of unfolding and loving enough to watch your created and changing world, a sharing of creative genius for patriarchs and matriarchs, prophets, priests and kings, and enough left over for hopes for more.

Thy kingdom come, thy will be done on earth as it is in heaven.

—then one day in a barn on one of our own fields, near a small town where common folk and restless beasts hovered and angels sang, it was done on earth what was willed in heaven. Mary had a baby and Joseph held her hand and we got a glimpse of who you are and where you yearn to live.

Give us this day our daily bread and forgive us our sins as we forgive those who sin against us.

—Help us to ask for no more, no less than what we need: basic things. Then let us seek others whose cupboards are bare and find a way to help them fill them with good things. Forgive us our sins of tuning-out and neglecting often, aware enough to find it amazing that we can breathe love where we couldn't before.

And lead us not into temptation, but deliver us from evil, for thine is the kingdom and the power and the glory forever. Amen

—Yours is that miraculous and unexpected kingdom where low is high and rich is poor and down is up. Save us from the temptation and the evil that become contagious when we get that reversed and lose what was and is, first and last, bold and beautiful.

Morning

Praise to you, God of grace, for the major party of your gospel, for raising dead sons and daughters to life and seating us at table after table with blessings heaped in front of our eyes.

We adore you, great God, because we have discovered that we are reconciled and restored not because we are thrifty, brave, clean and reverent, but because we were lost and have been found and our life is hid with Christ in you.

We come in awe realizing that the gospel is not ultimately about religion, mortality or any other solemn subject but really about your having great things in store, day in, day out, and you're just itching to share them with us. That feels like a huge celebration of new life, the best party ever thrown to which we respond enthusiastically, knowing it to be an open invitation to celebrate this new day in your world.

An Evening Prayer

Holy God and Lord of the evening and the going down of the sun, praise to you for your grand idea of letting earth and soul rest now, that on the other side of this night's gifts of quiet we may rise refreshed again.

Praise to you that amidst the frenzy and the fragile and the fragmented, you still hold steady the foundations of your world—seasons, stars, oceans, clouds, friends who remain faithful and salvation freely offered.

Before sleep enfolds us again tonight, hear our wide-ranging thoughts about your watch on the world and all our little worlds of relationships and daily tasks, and help us now to hand them over to you for a few hours, you who have promised to carry them when too heavy for us alone.

Advent

Holy and loving God, grant that these Advent days be reminders that you love your people less because of their merits than in spite of their unworthiness, when we find the unpacking of the old and wonderful story of redemption through the life and death of Jesus to be up-to-the-minute enough to fire us with anticipation.

We come again to the threshold of the day that is filled already with breathtaking and poignant images—a baby in a feeding trough, an overoccupied inn, pregnant Mary and anxious Joseph, grazing sheep and bright, angelic heavens. But let us be like children on tiptoe, that when the holy day of God in the flesh of Jesus comes crying into a bewildering world, we sing praises as men, women and children come to life again in him whose birth we sing.

Advent

Gracious, patient God in our waiting time, let this be a season of active waiting, not given too quickly to Christmas themes that we miss the opportunity to come alongside many who need to be loved in their waiting. That includes the jobless, waiting for the phone call that announces a hiring, the far-off village on the other side of the world waiting for the sight and sound of weapons to cease. Some would love to hear a word about peace and safety and that drug house nearby to come tumbling down.

Help us, before we get too caught up in our own Christmas joy, to make a place in our hearts for many for whom we might even become the only hint about a God who cared enough to come among us a disarming Baby Boy, a real hope, a redeemer of life's lost meaning.

Advent

God of promise, the mood of this day is both praise for great reminders of the long and wonder-filled story of salvation and a call from our own readiness to embrace Jesus who comes among us again.

Grant us the foresight to allow ourselves time before Christmas breaks in on our world to acknowledge the magnitude of the wrongs Jesus came to make right, the earnestness you look for so the joy we reap when the manger child arrives is not shallow or cheap.

Hear our desire to lift up our heads and hearts so room is prepared well during these days of anticipation.

Mid-Advent

Holy God, praise to you for Mary, blessed believer open to your magnificent gift of an unusual baby, free enough in her youth to be prophetic about the world-shaking news of your coming.

Here in mid-Advent when our barren lives show promise now and then that your holy light still shines in the various darknesses of human failure and sin's tenacious grasp, hear our hearts' confessions so we will have a more open place for the birthing of something, Someone new in this pregnant time.

Keep leaving your peace with us so we all keep participating with you in making this a peace-filled world, a love-filled world, a world open to the amazing grace that is always on its way.

Christmas

Wonderful Counselor, Mighty God, Prince of Peace, there are never enough gracious, loving and powerful names to shout today for the joy of our redemption arriving in our Savior Christ Jesus.

On this day when we cherish gifts given and received and dear ones sharing good food and drink at our celebrative tables, help us to hold in our hearts persons who find this day difficult to face. The year has perhaps brought grief from loss of a cherished life, rare occasions for any kind of festive table because relationships have turned hostile or financial securities have disappeared. Sons and daughters are on the other side of the world in the service of the country, and neighbors' children are caught in addictions and forfeiting their dreams.

So keep us in touch with both your amazing grace as faithful Savior always birthing new things for us, and with those for whom this is not a good time for rejoicing. Help us find ways to share the peace that comes in you and also avenues we can open for others to find it too.

Christmas Thanks

God of grace and God of glory, you who know, ever since we fell, that you wanted to bring us home again. Praise for Christmas, which always seems to come to us at the right time. For, at moments of birth we are reminded that all is potential and the future is open and promising.

We thank you for love, which came wrapped so graphically in the swaddling clothes of our Lord, the greatest gift for our deepest needs. By the birth of our Savior we are encouraged again as a great hope begins to rise like a lump in the throat, that you will ransom us and our world again from any darkness that seeks to destroy us. Light our way like the shining over Bethlehem so that on this day when joy is born we fear no dark night of sin and shame but, rather, find ourselves blessed with new dreams and visions.

Like Mary, who pondered and reflected nobly about what had changed her life and ours by the wonder of the Holy Spirit, help us take time today to invite your marvel again. Like Joseph, knowing

his life was strangely out of control and unpredict-
able, show us how to let go of treasured comforts
for the glory of whatever visit the Spirit is anxious
to make again.

Christmas Promise

No dreamer of ecstasies
poised to alarm, amaze
    an inoculated world,
    scarcely knowing the gnaw of its hunger;
No prophet of wonders
moved to judge and forewarn
    a minor people
    hardly confronting the scope of her need;

No singer of ballads
rehearsed to lift and enspirit
    a humbled nation,
    barely unleashing the grief of her
    bondage;

Could ever have dreamed
or foretold or composed
    the sign for their freedom
    arriving at night, silent as whisper;

A convergence of stars, bright,
observed by a few,

following, awestruck,
wonder of mystery, strong magnet of
promise;
A girl full-term, anxious,
bruised from the beast,
tired of travel,
hopeful of shelter, strong bearer of
destiny;

A drafty shed, dark, unlikely,
battered by age,
mangered times over,
odored by sheep, furnished for glory;
A Boy, infant arriving, longed-for,
promised by seers,
seeded by Spirit,
surrounded by angels, redeeming the
world!

Lent

Holy God, hear our prayers this Lenten season when
we acknowledge your patience with our rebellions
and ask that you would know and feel our repentance. For we acknowledge ourselves for what we
are and you for who you are, and we now yearn to
follow closely Jesus Christ. It is in his last work and

his last days that we face again our failure and the magnitude of your plan for our salvation.

We confess that knowing Jesus suffered, making it clear that nothing would stop him from loving the whole world, makes us conscious of our failure to do the same. You have shown us that the life that empties itself is the life to be prized, that in the long run the pain of self-indulgence is harder to bear than the pain of death.

Now in the season of the cross, we know that you would not have us know it as the unveiling of a horror story. Rather, you have shown it to be a place and time of high praise that the love that shook Eden's morning reigned on the tree and is shed abroad in all our hearts.

Lent

Cross-bearing Lord,

Come to all those places where the power of death would hold and force its way and say a redemptive word:

Where there is human wreckage, like those precious children of yours bombed out and foreclosed;

Where refugees and immigrants wonder where

next they will sleep and if anyone wants them anymore;

Where folks just like us on the world's other side are named enemies and who, like us, covet our mutual prayers;

Give us, in this holy and repentant time, a new vision of your weeping over our groaning creation, and stooping to our weakness of courage, offer surely as always your unconditional love and renewing Spirit.

And we will sing again the glory of the cross.

Lent

Jesus, friend of sinners, we are grateful that something so rich, so deep brings us inside each year at this time, away from the relentless cycle of getting things done in our world, into the nearness of the fires of our faith. For this is the time you have given us each yearly pilgrimage to get to the things that really matter in the formation of our soul's life.

Our praise, God, is for your Son, Jesus Christ, healer and reconciler, the one whose arms stretch down to lift us up, whose shepherd heart is with his sheep.

Our joy is in the telling again your story, that you have always loved us. In fact, the retelling from generation to generation hasn't spoiled the impact, that after long years of partnership with us belligerents, your decision to show your true colors in the suffering and death of Jesus is as new and bright as each morning's dawn.

So high above all our thanksgivings for this week's food and this month's health, we observe, dumbfounded and with ever-deeper gratitude, that you keep bearing our griefs, carrying our sorrows, visiting us in all the different "rooms" of our lives.

Lent

Holy God, Servant Lord, we are finding that this following servant Jesus, this wilderness and temptation-living, this cross-bearing and cross-taking is a risky and strange way to live in our culture. Your model of humility doesn't fit well into our categories. So thank you for showing us that we don't have to live and behave by everyone else's social rules. Thank you for not changing your mind on the mountain, at Galilee, in Gethsemane or on the cross. Thank you for loving us to the end, from beginning to the end.

When we are tempted to give you a list of things and changes we'd like you to give or make, remind us that what you only really give is your Spirit. We dare to believe that is what we need, and we're strong to affirm the faith that such is what we freely receive.

What wondrous love is this, O my soul!

Easter

God of wonderful surprises, thanks be to you for reminding us to be on alert for messages coming from unexpected places, remembering that Jesus came back first on Easter morning to a few friends trying to be customary in refreshing a grave.

Praise for your life-changing act of bringing the whole world back to you! Finding the tomb empty except for angels telling the wondrous truth, his best friends were soon to discover that their Jesus was giving them, and us, both a happy mystery and a future.

O God, we know death and loss are natural, but by your grace those heavy stones have been rolled away and the seed of life in us can never be killed. There is nothing we cannot do—move mountains, banish fear, love our enemies, change the world!

Easter

Great and loving God, the whole creation celebrates

today with the rich green rug of the fields and the yellows and purples of flowers spread in irregular embroidery on the earth. The sparkle of hope in each other's eyes today tops it all, giving praise that you never forget to fertilize your world each springtime so that it promises to bear both fruit and beauty again.

But the lift in the heart that shows in the eyes is because you make good today on your eternal pledge that we shall never die, that we are fueled again to yearn for life here and in eternity with you.

Let the children sense today that new clothes or special dinners with family are pointers to something more than spring. Let them know that we older folks are ecstatic about your dominion in the world and in heaven. And let us grown men and women have the childlike abandon to talk about it and live it today and always as inheritors of life's greatest prize.

Easter

Great God, who visits graves with hope and cathedrals with joy, let all the overflow of the good news of death's defeat wash and cleanse everything in its tide.

For if Easter is everything we know it to be, we treasure its potential to reverse the trend of life's defeats and destructions. We pray that old prejudices will die and bad memories will be healed and unforgiving attitudes will yield to all the possibilities of resurrection living.

Praise to you for the mystery that surrounds Easter morning news. Save us from trying to analyze it to pieces, so that we simply end up being great detectives and miss the freedom of fully embracing the joy and wonder of what you, O God, can do for your Son and for us on any surprising morning.

Easter

Risen Lord, the whole orchestra of the heart plays with an explosion of joy today. Trumpets sound like "alleluia" and cellos sing a warm sense of peace at last. Drums beat the rhythms of victory, and violins dialogue with oboes and flutes to raise our hopes and dreams to fever pitch. What a day, God, for you have again repeated the greatest surprise for the world to applaud, that death's flood has lost its chill since Jesus crossed the river!

Praise to you for this triumphant day, for sins forgiven, for promises of eternal life, for Scripture's re-assurances, for everything in your long history with us that has proven to be both dependable and true. Praise to you for Jesus Christ, risen, glorious and be-lievable, visible everywhere we look in those who love you and in those in whose weakness and pain we see your own suffering love.

So, praise for the great music of the heart and for the theme that keeps going, and going. Alleluia, alleluia.

Easter

It's a brand new day, Jesus,
    a shining Sunday that's just been born
    and has only twenty-four hours to live it up.
This day is a special one for me
    for no reason except that I choose to make
        it special
    and the choice is mine.
Today I want to tune into my feelings and
        accept them,
    to wake the joy that lies sleeping beneath a
        blanket of everydayness
    and say, "It's time to get up and celebrate—
    this is the Lord's day—and mine!"

I want to worship you, Lord, with all the
      stops out,
    to sing a hymn like I mean it for a change,
    to dance with tambourines and drums and
      shouts of joy,
      just like you told us to in olden days.
    I want to dance like David and pray like
      Paul
      and find out what hallelujah really
      means.
Help me to shake loose from my hang-ups
    and feel the freedom to be spontaneous
      and fully alive.
Today I want to go to church, unafraid to
      laugh or cry
    or show the human feelings that I hold
      inside.
And when the hour has ended, please make
      the meaning of it last.
Help me to be free to touch a stranger with
      my eyes without shyness,
    free to touch a lonely person with my
      hands in your name,
    free to do whatever I feel like doing that
      honors you.
I'd like to paint a prayer on a kite and fly it
      over Houston.

I wish I flew a plane so I could use the vapor
    trail to write,
  "I love you, Lord," across the sky.
I'd like to give bluebonnets to people I've
    never met
  and blackberries to people I've never liked
  and laughter to everyone.
I'd like to give my love and my life to you,
    Lord.

After Easter

Holy God, who in great love has bonded us to yourself in the selfless choice of offering up your Son
Jesus in our world, accept our praise for every time
and every place we find him risen and reigning
among us. For every time we resist the seduction of
power's many faces, every way we recognize surprises of grace where and when we had no hope nor
courage, we unashamedly credit our companion Jesus having taken room in our hearts.

All of which inspires our thanksgiving for things
routinely ours—breath, food, reasonable comforts
and fresh, daily gifts of spiritual miracles that keep
us going when so much around us threatens to per-
petuate anxiety and despair.

We pray that our prayers might be an encouragement to those suffering battle wounds, death encounters of war and war victims, strife on our city streets, violence and abuse in homes, to the end that knowing we are redeemed by a wounded Savior, we are all held by one who loves and understands like no other.

Pentecost

Mighty God, who loosed those many tongues and voices at Pentecost, help us to give voice to the many gifts and graces that announce our diversity and your wisdom.

Scripture says you gave some the gift to say wise things; we've noticed that some are especially compassionate and others are artists who awaken our senses and sensibilities. Teachers and preachers come to mind, engineers and carpenters, singers who can release our emotions profoundly, and doctors and nurses who help you heal tenderly. Thanks to you for the countless others and for me, gifted by you so that I can be uniquely who I am.

Praise to you, Holy Spirit, who challenge us to admire and assist in the blending of earth's many voices that one day they may all proclaim and cheer a common theme of thanksgiving and peace ecstatic.

Pentecost

Freshen us still, Holy Spirit, as you did one day when a crowd gathered in one place and were treated to a holy trembling of unusual and wonderful interruption.

And while your wind of grace sweeps us now, let it cool our torrid passions for greed, conflict and abuse of creation's splendid beauty. Rather, may that breeze comfort us in our anxieties, stir us to thanksgiving, awaken us from lethargy, and inspire us to passion for whatever breeds freedom, love and compassion for all of your children everywhere.

We confess our part in fostering unnecessary attachment to old ways of doing things and doubting that you could really stir our imaginations to the changes that placing ourselves in the path of your whisper and gale might bring.

Pentecost

The wind of the Spirit is blowing,
    lift me, Lord, and let me soar with the
        speed of time,

content to see the dust of yesterday bury
    the past.
Chase the wind with me,
Dream with me,
Yesterday is gone and can't be held by wishes.
Now is the time for vision and for prayer,
This is a day for new adventures
    I do rejoice,
       and I am glad.

Thanksgiving Day

Amazing good and gracious God, today we offer up psalms and hymns of deep thanksgiving not because you need offerings or sacrifice or even our praise, but so our vision, often preoccupied by things close at hand and cut down in size, may focus on greatness, eternity and your endless supply of exactly what we need.

We give you thanks for the vision that those of faith have brought to this land of ours. For the Native Americans here long before we arrived who keep teaching us to live at peace with your earth. Remind us by their presence how dependent we are upon your created order.

We thank you for women and men of color who

came shackled and bound, who have given us a legacy of hope and determination. With them let us not flag in zeal for a society free of racism, bigotry and hate.

Praise for bread at our tables, friends who love us, for winter sparrows, for singers and doctors, teachers and dreamers, children who sing and smile out of a four- or five-year-old heart, for the church alive in your world.

Keep us faithful, hopeful, and restless with the world's injustices, and keep us clothed in the bright colors of risk and adventure for you.

PRAYING THE SCRIPTURES

❧

Addiction

I lift up my eyes to the mountains—
    where does my help come from?
My help comes from the LORD,
    the Maker of heaven and earth.

He will not let your foot slip—
    he who watches over you will not
       slumber. . . .

The LORD will keep you from all harm—
    he will watch over your life;
the LORD will watch over your coming and going
    both now and forevermore.
PSALM 121:1-3, 7-8 NIV

• • •

I lift up my eyes to the hills—
    from where will my help come?

My help comes from the LORD,
    who made heaven and earth.
He will not let your foot be moved;
    he who keeps you will not slumber. . . .

The LORD will keep you from all evil;
    he will keep your life.
The LORD will keep your going out and your
        coming in
from this time on and forevermore.
PSALM 121:1-3, 7-8 NRSV

• • •

I look up to the mountains; does my strength
        come from mountains?
    No, my strength comes from God,
        who made heaven, and earth, and
        mountains.
He won't let you stumble,
    your Guardian God won't fall asleep. . . .

GOD guards you from every evil,
    he guards your very life.
He guards you when you leave and when you
        return,
    he guards you now, he guards you always.
PSALM 121:1-3, 7-8 *The Message*

• • •

Out of the depths I cry to you, O LORD.

Lord, hear my voice!
Let your ears be attentive
    to the voice of my supplications!
If you, O LORD, should mark iniquities,
    Lord, who could stand?
But there is forgiveness with you,
    so that you may be revered.

I wait for the LORD, my soul waits,
    and in his word I hope;
my soul waits for the Lord
    more than those who watch for the
        morning,
    more than those who watch for the
        morning.

O Israel, hope in the LORD!
    For with the LORD there is steadfast love,
    and with him is great power to redeem.
It is he who will redeem Israel
    from all its iniquities.

PSALM 130 NRSV

• • •

Help, GOD—the bottom has fallen out of my
      life! Master, hear my cry for help!
    Listen hard! Open your ears!
      Listen to my cries for mercy.

If you, GOD, kept records on wrongdoings,

who would stand a chance?
As it turns out, forgiveness is your habit,
    and that's why you're worshiped.

I pray to God—my life a prayer—
    and wait for what he'll say and do.
My life's on the line before God, my Lord,
    waiting and watching till morning,
    waiting and watching till morning.

O Israel, wait and watch for God—
    with God's arrival comes love,
    with God's arrival comes generous
        redemption.
No doubt about it—he'll redeem Israel,
    buy back Israel from captivity to sin.
Psalm 130 *The Message*

.   .   .

For I am convinced that neither death nor life,
neither angels nor demons, neither the present nor
the future, nor any powers, neither height nor depth,
nor anything else in all creation, will be able to separate us from the love of God that is in Christ Jesus
our Lord.
Romans 8:38-39 niv

.   .   .

For I am convinced that neither death, nor life,

nor angels, nor rulers, nor things present, nor things
to come, nor powers, nor height, nor depth, nor anything else in all creation, will be able to separate us
from the love of God in Christ Jesus our Lord.
Romans 8:38-39 nrsv

. . .

I'm absolutely convinced that nothing—nothing
living or dead, angelic or demonic, today or tomorrow, high or low, thinkable or unthinkable—absolutely nothing can get between us and God's love
because of the way that Jesus our Master has embraced us.
Romans 8:38-39 *The Message*

. . .

Others
Psalm 46
Isaiah 63:7-9
Matthew 15:21-28
2 Corinthians 4:6-9
Galatians 2:20

Aging

I will bless the Lord at all times;
    his praise shall continually be in my
        mouth.

My soul makes its boast in the LORD;
　　let the humble hear and be glad.
O magnify the LORD with me,
　　and let us exalt his name together.

I sought the LORD, and he answered me,
　　and delivered me from all my fears.
Look to him, and be radiant;
　　so your faces shall never be ashamed.
This poor soul cried, and was heard by the LORD,
　　and was saved from every trouble.
The angel of the LORD encamps
　　around those who fear him, and delivers them.
O taste and see that the LORD is good;
　　happy are those who take refuge in him.
PSALM 34:1-8 NRSV

•　•　•

I bless GOD every chance I get; my lungs
　　　　expand with his praise.
I live and breathe GOD;
　　if things aren't going well, hear this and be
　　　　happy:

Join me in spreading the news;
　　together let's get the word out.

GOD met me more than halfway,
　　he freed me from my anxious fears.

Look at him; give him your warmest smile.
    Never hide your feelings from him.
When I was desperate, I called out,
    and GOD got me out of a tight spot.

GOD's angel sets up a circle
    of protection around us while we pray.

Open your mouth and taste, open your eyes
            and see—
        how good GOD is.
Blessed are you who run to him.
PSALM 34:1-8 *The Message*

         • • •

For you, O Lord, are my hope,
    my trust, O LORD, from my youth.
Upon you I have leaned from my birth;
    it was you who took me from my mother's
        womb.
My praise is continually of you. . . .

So even to old age and gray hairs,
    O God, do not forsake me,
until I proclaim your might
    to all the generations to come.
Your power and your righteousness, O God,
    reach the high heavens.
You who have done great things,
    O God, who is like you?

You who have made me see many troubles
    and calamities
  will revive me again;
from the depths of the earth
  you will bring me up again.
You will increase my honor,
  and comfort me once again.

I will also praise you with the harp
  for your faithfulness, O my God;
I will sing praises to you with the lyre,
  O Holy One of Israel.
My lips will shout for joy
  when I sing praises to you;
  my soul also, which you have rescued.
PSALM 71:5-6, 18-23 NRSV

• • •

You keep me going when times are tough—
  my bedrock, GOD, since my childhood.
I've hung on you from the day of my birth,
  the day you took me from the cradle;
  I'll never run out of praise. . . .
I'll keep at it until I'm old and gray.
  God, don't walk off and leave me
  until I get out the news
Of your strong right arm to this world,
  news of your power to the world yet to
    come,

Your famous and righteous
    ways, O God.
God, you've done it all!
    Who is quite like you?
You, who made me stare trouble in the face,
    Turn me around;
Now let me look life in the face.
    I've been to the bottom;
Bring me up, streaming with honors;
    turn to me, be tender to me,
And I'll take up the lute and thank you
    to the tune of your faithfulness, God.
I'll make music for you on a harp,
    Holy One of Israel.
When I open up in song to you,
    I let out lungsful of praise,
    my rescued life a song.
PSALM 71:5-6, 18-23 *The Message*

• • •

I thank my God every time I remember you, constantly praying with joy in every one of my prayers for all of you, because of your sharing in the gospel from the first day until now. I am confident of this, that the one who began a good work among you will bring it to completion by the day of Jesus Christ.

It is right for me to think this way about all of

you, because you hold me in your heart, for all of you share in God's grace with me, both in my imprisonment and in the defense and confirmation of the gospel.

PHILIPPIANS 1:3-7 NRSV

. . .

Every time you cross my mind, I break out in exclamations of thanks to God. Each exclamation is a trigger to prayer. I find myself praying for you with a glad heart. I am so pleased that you have continued on in this with us, believing and proclaiming God's Message, from the day you heard it right up to the present. There has never been the slightest doubt in my mind that the God who started this great work in you would keep at it and bring it to a flourishing finish on the very day Christ Jesus appears.

It's not at all fanciful for me to think this way about you. My prayers and hopes have deep roots in reality. You have, after all, stuck with me all the way from the time I was thrown in jail, put on trial, and came out of it in one piece. All along you have experienced with me the most generous help from God.

PHILIPPIANS 1:3-7 *The Message*

. . .

Others

Psalm 27:1, 5-7, 13-14

Psalm 42:1-8

Psalm 91

Psalm 121

Lamentations 3:33-34

Romans 8:22-23

1 Peter 1:13-15

Anger, Bitterness, Self-Pity

> I will extol you, O LORD, for you have drawn
>   me up,
>   and did not let my foes rejoice over me.
> O LORD my God, I cried to you for help,
>   and you have healed me.
> O LORD, you brought up my soul from Sheol,
>   restored me to life from among those gone
>   down to the Pit.
>
> Sing praises to the LORD, O you his faithful ones,
>   and give thanks to his holy name.
> For his anger is but for a moment;
>   his favor is for a lifetime.
> Weeping may linger for the night,
>   but joy comes with the morning.
>
> As for me, I said in my prosperity,

"I shall never be moved."
By your favor, O LORD, you had established
          me as a strong mountain;
     you hid your face; I was dismayed.

To you, O LORD, I cried,
     and to the LORD I made supplication:
"What profit is there in my death,
     if I go down to the Pit?
Will the dust praise you?
     Will it tell of your faithfulness?
Hear, O LORD, and be gracious to me!
     O LORD, be my helper!"

You have turned my mourning into dancing;
     you have taken off my sackcloth
     and clothed me with joy,
so that my soul may praise you and not be
          silent.
     O LORD my God, I will give thanks to you
          forever.

PSALM 30 NRSV

• • •

I give you all the credit, GOD— you got me
          out of that mess,
     you didn't let my foes gloat.

GOD, my God, I yelled for help
     and you put me together.

GOD, you pulled me out of the grave,
    gave me another chance at life
    when I was down-and-out.

All you saints! Sing your hearts out to GOD!
    Thank him to his face!
He gets angry once in a while, but across
    a lifetime there is only love.
The nights of crying your eyes out
    give way to days of laughter.

When things were going great
    I crowed, "I've got it made.
I'm GOD's favorite.
    He made me king of the mountain."
Then you looked the other way
    and I fell to pieces.

I called out to you, GOD;
    I laid my case before you:
"Can you sell me for a profit when I'm dead?
    auction me off at a cemetery yard sale?
When I'm 'dust to dust' my songs
    and stories of you won't sell.
So listen! and be kind!
    Help me out of this!"

You did it: you changed wild lament
    into whirling dance;

You ripped off my black mourning band
    and decked me with wildflowers.
I'm about to burst with song;
    I can't keep quiet about you.
GOD, my God,
    I can't thank you enough.
PSALM 30 *The Message*

    • • •

Where can I go from your spirit?
    Or where can I flee from your presence?
If I ascend to heaven, you are there;
    if I make my bed in Sheol, you are there.
If I take the wings of the morning
    and settle at the farthest limits of the sea,
even there your hand shall lead me,
    and your right hand shall hold me fast.
If I say, "Surely the darkness shall cover me,
    and the light around me become night,"
even the darkness is not dark to you;
    the night is as bright as the day,
    for darkness is as light to you.
PSALM 139:7-12 NRSV

    • • •

Is there anyplace I can go to avoid your
        Spirit?
    to be out of your sight?
If I climb to the sky, you're there!

> If I go underground, you're there!
> If I flew on morning's wings
>   to the far western horizon,
> You'd find me in a minute—
>   you're already there waiting!
> Then I said to myself, "Oh, he even sees me in
>   the dark!
>   At night I'm immersed in the light!"
> It's a fact: darkness isn't dark to you;
>   night and day, darkness and light, they're
>   all the same to you.
> PSALM 139:7-12 *The Message*

• • •

Others

Psalm 39

Isaiah 53

Matthew 26:36-46

1 Corinthians 13

2 Corinthians 1:3-7

Philippians 2:5-11

1 Peter 5:6-11

Bereavement, Grief

> O that my words were written down!
>   O that they were inscribed in a book!

O that with an iron pen and with lead
    they were engraved on a rock forever!
For I know that my Redeemer lives,
    and that at the last he will stand upon the
        earth;
and after my skin has been thus destroyed,
    then in my flesh I shall see God,

JOB 19:23-26 NRSV

· · ·

If only my words were written in a book—
    better yet, chiseled in stone!
Still, I know that God lives—the One who
    gives me back my life—
    and eventually he'll take his stand on earth.
And I'll see him—even though I get skinned
    alive!

JOB 19:23-26 *The Message*

· · ·

On this mountain the LORD of hosts will make
    for all peoples
    a feast of rich food, a feast of well-aged
      wines,
    of rich food filled with marrow, of well-
      aged wines strained clear.

And he will destroy on this mountain
    the shroud that is cast over all peoples,
    the sheet that is spread over all nations;

he will swallow up death forever.
Then the Lord GOD will wipe away the tears
     from all faces,
  and the disgrace of his people he will take
    away from all the earth,
  for the LORD has spoken.
It will be said on that day,
  Lo, this is our God; we have waited for
    him, so that he might save us.
  This is the LORD for whom we have waited;
  let us be glad and rejoice in his salvation.
ISAIAH 25:6-9 NRSV

· · ·

But here on this mountain,
    God-of-the-Angel-Armies
  will throw a feast for all the people of the
    world,
A feast of the finest foods, a feast with vintage
    wines,
  a feast of seven courses, a feast lavish with
    gourmet desserts.
And here on this mountain, God will banish
  the pall of doom hanging over all peoples,
The shadow of doom darkening all nations.
  Yes, he'll banish death forever.
And God will wipe the tears from every face.
  He'll remove every sign of disgrace

From his people, wherever they are.
>   Yes! God says so!

Also at that time, people will say,
>   "Look at what's happened! This is our God!
We waited for him and he showed up and
>   saved us!
>   This God, the one we waited for!
Let's celebrate, sing the joys of his salvation."
ISAIAH 25:6-9 *The Message*

· · ·

The steadfast love of the LORD never ceases, his mercies never come to an end; they are new every morning; great is your faithfulness. . . . For the Lord will not reject forever. Although he causes grief, he will have compassion according to the abundance of his steadfast love; for he does not willingly afflict or grieve anyone. . . . I called on your name, O LORD, from the depths of the pit; you heard my plea, "Do not close your ear to my cry for help, but give me relief!" You came near when I called on you; you said, "Do not fear!"

LAMENTATIONS 3:22-23, 31-33, 55-57 NRSV

· · ·

God's loyal love couldn't have run out,
>   his merciful love couldn't have dried up.

They're created new every morning.
   How great your faithfulness! . . .
Why? Because the Master won't ever
   walk out and fail to return.
If he works severely, he also works tenderly.
   His stockpiles of loyal love are immense.
He takes no pleasure in making life hard,
   in throwing roadblocks in the way: . . .
I called out your name, O God,
   called from the bottom of the pit.
You listened when I called out, "Don't shut
     your ears!
   Get me out of here! Save me!"
You came close when I called out.
   You said, "It's going to be all right."
LAMENTATIONS 3:22-23, 31-33, 55-57 *The Message*

• • •

Therefore, since we are justified by faith, we have peace with God through our Lord Jesus Christ, through whom we have obtained access to this grace in which we stand; and we boast in our hope of sharing the glory of God. And not only that, but we also boast in our sufferings, knowing that suffering produces endurance, and endurance produces character, and character produces hope, and hope does not disappoint us, because God's love has been poured into our hearts through the

Holy Spirit that has been given to us.

For while we were still weak, at the right time Christ died for the ungodly. Indeed, rarely will anyone die for a righteous person—though perhaps for a good person someone might actually dare to die. But God proves his love for us in that while we still were sinners Christ died for us. Much more surely then, now that we have been justified by his blood, will we be saved through him from the wrath of God. For if while we were enemies, we were reconciled to God through the death of his Son, much more surely, having been reconciled, will we be saved by his life. But more than that, we even boast in God through our Lord Jesus Christ, through whom we have now received reconciliation.

ROMANS 5:1-11 NRSV

• • •

By entering through faith into what God has always wanted to do for us—set us right with him, make us fit for him—we have it all together with God because of our Master Jesus. And that's not all: We throw open our doors to God and discover at the same moment that he has already thrown open his door to us. We find ourselves standing where we always hoped we might stand—out in the wide open spaces of God's grace and glory, standing tall and shouting our praise.

There's more to come: We continue to shout our praise even when we're hemmed in with troubles, because we know how troubles can develop passionate patience in us, and how that patience in turn forges the tempered steel of virtue, keeping us alert for whatever God will do next. In alert expectancy such as this, we're never left feeling shortchanged. Quite the contrary—we can't round up enough containers to hold everything God generously pours into our lives through the Holy Spirit!

Christ arrives right on time to make this happen. He didn't, and doesn't, wait for us to get ready. He presented himself for this sacrificial death when we were far too weak and rebellious to do anything to get ourselves ready. And even if we hadn't been so weak, we wouldn't have known what to do anyway. We can understand someone dying for a person worth dying for, and we can understand how someone good and noble could inspire us to selfless sacrifice. But God put his love on the line for us by offering his Son in sacrificial death while we were of no use whatever to him.

Now that we are set right with God by means of this sacrificial death, the consummate blood sacrifice, there is no longer a question of being at odds with God in any way. If, when we were at our worst, we were put on friendly terms with God by the sacrificial death of his Son, now that we're at our best, just think of how our lives will expand and deepen by means of his resurrection life! Now that we have actually received this amazing friendship with God, we are no longer content to simply say it in plodding prose. We sing and shout our praises to God through Jesus, the Messiah!

ROMANS 5:1-11 *The Message*

• • •

Others

Isaiah 61:1-3

Matthew 11:28-30

John 6:37-40

John 14:1-6

Romans 5:17-21

Romans 6:3-9

Romans 8:31-35, 37-39

Romans 14:7-9

1 Corinthians 15:12-16

Philippians 3:20-21

1 Thessalonians 4:13-18

1 Peter 1:3-5

1 John 3:1-2

Revelation 21:1-7

Childbirth

LORD, our Lord,
    how majestic is your name in all the earth!

You have set your glory
    above the heavens.
Through the praise of children and infants
    you have established a stronghold against
        your enemies,
    to silence the foe and the avenger.
When I consider your heavens, the work of
        your fingers,
    the moon and the stars, which you have set
        in place,
what are mere mortals that you are mindful of
        them,
    human beings that you care for them?

You have made them a little lower than the
        angels
and crowned them with glory and honor.

You made them rulers over the works of your
        hands;
    you put everything under their feet:

all flocks and herds,
    and the animals of the wild,
the birds in the sky,
    and the fish in the sea,
    all that swim the paths of the seas.

LORD, our Lord,
how majestic is your name in all the earth!
PSALM 8 NIV

• • •

O LORD, you have searched me and known me.
You know when I sit down and when I rise up;
    you discern my thoughts from far away. . . .
For it was you who formed my inward parts;
    you knit me together in my mother's womb.
I praise you, for I am fearfully and wonder-
        fully made.
    Wonderful are your works;
that I know very well.
    My frame was not hidden from you,
when I was being made in secret,
    intricately woven in the depths of the earth.
Your eyes beheld my unformed substance.
In your book were written

all the days that were formed for me,
when none of them as yet existed.
How weighty to me are your thoughts, O God!
    How vast is the sum of them!
I try to count them—they are more than the sand;
    I come to the end—I am still with you.
Psalm 139:1-2, 13-18 nrsv

· · ·

God, investigate my life; get all the facts
    firsthand.
    I'm an open book to you;
    even from a distance, you know what I'm
        thinking. . . .
Oh yes, you shaped me first inside, then out;
    you formed me in my mother's womb.
I thank you, High God—you're breathtaking!
    Body and soul, I am marvelously made!
    I worship in adoration—what a creation!
You know me inside and out,
    you know every bone in my body;
You know exactly how I was made, bit by bit,
    how I was sculpted from nothing into
        something.
Like an open book, you watched me grow
        from conception to birth;
    all the stages of my life were spread out
        before you,

The days of my life all prepared
    before I'd even lived one day.

Your thoughts—how rare, how beautiful!
    God, I'll never comprehend them!
I couldn't even begin to count them—
    any more than I could count the sand of
        the sea.
Oh, let me rise in the morning and live always
    with you!

PSALM 139:1-2, 13-18 *The Message*

• • •

People were also bringing babies to Jesus for him to place his hands on them. When the disciples saw this, they rebuked them. But Jesus called the children to him and said, "Let the little children come to me, and do not hinder them, for the kingdom of God belongs to such as these. Truly I tell you, anyone who will not receive the kingdom of God like a little child will never enter it."

LUKE 18:15-17 NIV

• • •

Others

Psalm 100

Psalm 139:1-16

Ecclesiastes 11:5

Luke 1:39-55

Death Approaching

The LORD is my shepherd, I shall not want.
   He makes me lie down in green pastures;

he leads me beside still waters;
   he restores my soul.
He leads me in right paths
   for his name's sake.

Even though I walk through the darkest valley,
   I fear no evil;
for you are with me;
   your rod and your staff—
   they comfort me.

You prepare a table before me
   in the presence of my enemies;
you anoint my head with oil;
   my cup overflows.
Surely goodness and mercy shall follow me
   all the days of my life,
and I shall dwell in the house of the LORD
   my whole life long.

PSALM 23 NRSV

• • •

GOD, my shepherd! I don't need a thing.
   You have bedded me down in lush
      meadows,

you find me quiet pools to drink from.
True to your word,
>you let me catch my breath
>and send me in the right direction.

Even when the way goes through
>Death Valley,
I'm not afraid
>when you walk at my side.
Your trusty shepherd's crook
>makes me feel secure.

You serve me a six-course dinner
>right in front of my enemies.
You revive my drooping head;
>my cup brims with blessing.
Your beauty and love chase after me
>every day of my life.
I'm back home in the house of GOD
>for the rest of my life.
PSALM 23 *The Message*

• • •

For my Father's will is that everyone who looks to the Son and believes in him shall have eternal life, and I will raise them up at the last day.

Very truly I tell you, whoever believes has eternal life. I am the bread of life. Your ancestors ate the manna in the wilderness, yet they died. But here is the bread that comes down from heaven, which people may eat and not die. I am the living bread that came down from heaven. Whoever eats this bread will live forever. This bread is my flesh, which I will give for the life of the world.

John 6:40, 47-51 NIV

. . .

Do not let your hearts be troubled. Believe in God, believe also in me. In my Father's house there are many dwelling places. If it were not so, would I have told you that I go to prepare a place for you? And if I go and prepare a place for you, I will come again and will take you to myself, so that where I am, there you may be also.

John 14:1-3 NRSV

. . .

Don't let this throw you. You trust God, don't you? Trust me. There is plenty of room for you in my Father's home. If that weren't so, would I have told you that I'm on my way to get a room ready for you? And if I'm on my way to get your room ready, I'll come back and get you so you can live where I live.

John 14:1-3 *The Message*

. . .

Others

Psalm 31:5

Matthew 25:34

John 3:16-21

Romans 8:28-39

Romans 14:8

1 Corinthians 15:12-20

2 Corinthians 4:7-18

2 Corinthians 5:1

Philippians 3:7-14

1 Thessalonians 4:17

1 John 3:2

Revelation 7:9-17

Revelation 21:1-7, 22–22:5

Depression, Anxiety, Fear

God is our refuge and strength,
    a very present help in trouble.
Therefore we will not fear, though the earth
        should change,
    though the mountains shake in the heart of
        the sea;
though its waters roar and foam,
    though the mountains tremble with its
        tumult. *Selah*

There is a river whose streams make glad the
city of God,
the holy habitation of the Most High.
God is in the midst of the city; it shall not be
moved;
God will help it when the morning dawns.
The nations are in an uproar, the kingdoms
totter;
he utters his voice, the earth melts.

The LORD of hosts is with us;
the God of Jacob is our refuge. *Selah*

Come, behold the works of the LORD;
see what desolations he has brought on the
earth.
He makes wars cease to the end of the earth;
he breaks the bow, and shatters the spear;
he burns the shields with fire.
"Be still, and know that I am God!
I am exalted among the nations,
I am exalted in the earth."
The LORD of hosts is with us;
the God of Jacob is our refuge. *Selah*
PSALM 46 NRSV

• • •

God is a safe place to hide,
ready to help when we need him.

We stand fearless at the cliff-edge of doom,
        courageous in seastorm and earthquake,
Before the rush and roar of oceans,
        the tremors that shift mountains.

Jacob-wrestling God fights for us,
        God-of-Angel-Armies protects us.

River fountains splash joy, cooling God's city,
        this sacred haunt of the Most High.
God lives here, the streets are safe,
        God at your service from crack of dawn.
Godless nations rant and rave, kings and
            kingdoms threaten,
        but Earth does anything he says.

Jacob-wrestling God fights for us,
        God-of-Angel-Armies protects us.
Attention, all! See the marvels of God!
        He plants flowers and trees all over the earth,
Bans war from pole to pole,
        breaks all the weapons across his knee.
        "Step out of the traffic! Take a long,
            loving look at me, your High God,
            above politics, above everything."

Jacob-wrestling God fights for us,
        God-of-Angel-Armies protects us.
Psalm 46 *The Message*

•   •   •

Cast your burden on the LORD,
   and he will sustain you;
he will never permit
   the righteous to be moved.
PSALM 55:22 NRSV

. . .

Pile your troubles on GOD's shoulders—
   He'll carry your load, he'll help you out.
He'll never let good people
   topple into ruin.
PSALM 55:22 *The Message*

. . .

When I am afraid,
   I put my trust in you.
In God, whose word I praise,
   in God I trust; I am not afraid;
   what can flesh do to me?
PSALM 56:3-4 NRSV

. . .

When I get really afraid
   I come to you in trust.
I'm proud to praise God;
   fearless now, I trust in God.
   What can mere mortals do?
PSALM 56:3-4 *The Message*

. . .

But now, this is what the LORD says—

he who created you, Jacob,
he who formed you, Israel:
"Do not fear, for I have redeemed you;
    I have summoned you by name; you are
        mine.
When you pass through the waters,
    I will be with you;
and when you pass through the rivers,
    they will not sweep over you.
When you walk through the fire,
    you will not be burned;
    the flames will not set you ablaze.
For I am the Lord your God,
    the Holy One of Israel, your Savior."
ISAIAH 43:1-3 NIV

• • •

Therefore I tell you, do not worry about your life, what you will eat or drink; or about your body, what you will wear. Is not life more important than food, and the body more important than clothes? Look at the birds of the air; they do not sow or reap or store away in barns, and yet your heavenly Father feeds them. Are you not much more valuable than they? Can any one of you by worrying add a single hour to your life?

And why do you worry about clothes? See how the flowers of the field grow. They do not labor or spin.

Yet I tell you that not even Solomon in all his splendor was dressed like one of these. If that is how God clothes the grass of the field, which is here today and tomorrow is thrown into the fire, will he not much more clothe you—you of little faith? So do not worry, saying, 'What shall we eat?' or 'What shall we drink?' or 'What shall we wear?' For the pagans run after all these things, and your heavenly Father knows that you need them. But seek first his kingdom and his righteousness, and all these things will be given to you as well. Therefore do not worry about tomorrow, for tomorrow will worry about itself. Each day has enough trouble of its own.

MATTHEW 6:25-34 NIV

• • •

Rejoice in the Lord always; again I will say, Rejoice. Let your gentleness be known to everyone. The Lord is near. Do not worry about anything, but in everything by prayer and supplication with thanksgiving let your requests be made known to God. And the peace of God, which surpasses all understanding, will guard your hearts and your minds in Christ Jesus.

PHILIPPIANS 4:4-7 NRSV

• • •

Celebrate God all day, every day. I mean, revel in him! Make it as clear as you can to all you meet that you're on their side, working with them and not against them. Help them see that the Master is about to arrive. He could show up any minute!

Don't fret or worry. Instead of worrying, pray. Let petitions and praises shape your worries into prayers, letting God know your concerns. Before you know it, a sense of God's wholeness, everything coming together for good, will come and settle you down. It's wonderful what happens when Christ displaces worry at the center of your life.

PHILIPPIANS 4:4-7 *The Message*

· · ·

Others

Psalm 27

Isaiah 35

Lamentations 3:55-58

John 10:1-18

John 14:1-6

Romans 8:31-35, 37-39

Gratitude

O LORD, our Sovereign,
    how majestic is your name in all the earth!

You have set your glory above the heavens.
   Out of the mouths of babes and infants
you have founded a bulwark because of your foes,
   to silence the enemy and the avenger.

When I look at your heavens, the work of
     your fingers,
the moon and the stars that you have
     established;
what are human beings that you are mindful
     of them,
   mortals that you care for them?

Yet you have made them a little lower than God,
   and crowned them with glory and honor.
You have given them dominion over the
     works of your hands;
   you have put all things under their feet,
all sheep and oxen,
   and also the beasts of the field,
the birds of the air, and the fish of the sea,
   whatever passes along the paths of the seas.
O LORD, our Sovereign,
   how majestic is your name in all the earth!
PSALM 8 NRSV

• • •

GOD, brilliant Lord, yours is a household
     name.

Nursing infants gurgle choruses about you;
    toddlers shout the songs
That drown out enemy talk,
    and silence atheist babble.

I look up at your macro-skies, dark and
        enormous,
    your handmade sky-jewelry,
Moon and stars mounted in their settings.
    Then I look at my micro-self and wonder,
Why do you bother with us?
    Why take a second look our way?

Yet we've so narrowly missed being gods,
    bright with Eden's dawn light.
You put us in charge of your handcrafted world,
    repeated to us your Genesis-charge,
Made us lords of sheep and cattle,
    even animals out in the wild,
Birds flying and fish swimming,
    whales singing in the ocean deeps.

God, brilliant Lord,
    your name echoes around the world.
Psalm 8 *The Message*

• • •

I will extol the Lord at all times;
    his praise will always be on my lips.
I will glory in the Lord;

let the afflicted hear and rejoice.
Glorify the LORD with me;
    let us exalt his name together.

I sought the LORD, and he answered me;
    he delivered me from all my fears.
Those who look to him are radiant;
    their faces are never covered with shame.
This poor man called, and the LORD heard him;
    he saved him out of all his troubles.
The angel of the LORD encamps around those
      who fear him,
    and he delivers them.

Taste and see that the LORD is good;
    blessed are those who take refuge in him.
PSALM 34:1-8 NIV

• • •

I will bless the LORD at all times;
    his praise shall continually be in my mouth.
My soul makes its boast in the LORD;
    let the humble hear and be glad.
O magnify the LORD with me,
    and let us exalt his name together.

I sought the LORD, and he answered me,
    and delivered me from all my fears.
Look to him, and be radiant;
    so your faces shall never be ashamed.

This poor soul cried, and was heard by the
     LORD,
   and was saved from every trouble.
The angel of the LORD encamps
   around those who fear him, and delivers them.
O taste and see that the LORD is good;
   happy are those who take refuge in him.
O fear the LORD, you his holy ones,
   for those who fear him have no want.
The young lions suffer want and hunger, but
     those who seek the LORD lack no good
     thing. . . .
When the righteous cry for help, the LORD
     hears,
   and rescues them from all their troubles.
The LORD is near to the brokenhearted,
   and saves the crushed in spirit.
PSALM 34:1-10, 17-18 NRSV

• • •

I bless GOD every chance I get;
   my lungs expand with his praise.

I live and breathe GOD;
   if things aren't going well, hear this and be
     happy:

Join me in spreading the news;
   together let's get the word out.

GOD met me more than halfway,
    he freed me from my anxious fears.

Look at him; give him your warmest smile.
    Never hide your feelings from him.

When I was desperate, I called out,
    and GOD got me out of a tight spot.

GOD's angel sets up a circle
    of protection around us while we pray.

Open your mouth and taste, open your eyes
        and see—
    how good GOD is.
Blessed are you who run to him.

Worship GOD if you want the best;
    worship opens doors to all his goodness.
Young lions on the prowl get hungry,
    but GOD-seekers are full of God. . . .
Is anyone crying for help? GOD is listening,
    ready to rescue you.

If your heart is broken, you'll find GOD right
        there;
    if you're kicked in the gut, he'll help you
        catch your breath.
PSALM 34:1-10, 17-18 *The Message*

• • •

Bless the LORD, O my soul,
  and all that is within me,
  bless his holy name.
Bless the LORD, O my soul,
  and do not forget all his benefits—
who forgives all your iniquity,
  who heals all your diseases,
who redeems your life from the Pit,
  who crowns you with steadfast love and
      mercy,
who satisfies you with good as long as you live
  so that your youth is renewed like the eagle's.

The LORD works vindication
  and justice for all who are oppressed.
He made known his ways to Moses,
  his acts to the people of Israel.
The LORD is merciful and gracious,
  slow to anger and abounding in steadfast
      love.
He will not always accuse,
  nor will he keep his anger forever.
He does not deal with us according to our sins,
  nor repay us according to our iniquities.
For as the heavens are high above the earth,
  so great is his steadfast love toward those
      who fear him;
as far as the east is from the west,

so far he removes our transgressions from us.
As a father has compassion for his children,
    so the LORD has compassion for those who
        fear him.
For he knows how we were made;
    he remembers that we are dust.

As for mortals, their days are like grass;
    they flourish like a flower of the field;
for the wind passes over it, and it is gone,
    and its place knows it no more.
But the steadfast love of the LORD is from
        everlasting to everlasting
    on those who fear him,
    and his righteousness to children's
        children,
to those who keep his covenant
    and remember to do his commandments.

The LORD has established his throne in the
        heavens,
    and his kingdom rules over all.
Bless the LORD, O you his angels,
    you mighty ones who do his bidding,
    obedient to his spoken word.
Bless the LORD, all his hosts,
    his ministers that do his will.
Bless the LORD, all his works,

in all places of his dominion.
Bless the LORD, O my soul.
PSALM 103 NRSV

· · ·

O my soul, bless GOD. From head to toe, I'll
     bless his holy name!
O my soul, bless GOD,
    don't forget a single blessing!

He forgives your sins—every one.
    He heals your diseases—every one.
    He redeems you from hell—saves your life!
    He crowns you with love and mercy—a
      paradise crown.
    He wraps you in goodness—beauty eternal.
    He renews your youth—you're always
      young in his presence.

God makes everything come out right;
    he puts victims back on their feet.
He showed Moses how he went about his work,
    opened up his plans to all Israel.
God is sheer mercy and grace;
    not easily angered, he's rich in love.
He doesn't endlessly nag and scold,
    nor hold grudges forever.
He doesn't treat us as our sins deserve,
    nor pay us back in full for our wrongs.

As high as heaven is over the earth,
  so strong is his love to those who fear him.
And as far as sunrise is from sunset,
  he has separated us from our sins.
As parents feel for their children,
  God feels for those who fear him.
He knows us inside and out,
  keeps in mind that we're made of mud.
Men and women don't live very long;
  like wildflowers they spring up and blossom,
But a storm snuffs them out just as quickly,
  leaving nothing to show they were here.
God's love, though, is ever and always,
  eternally present to all who fear him,
Making everything right for them and their
      children
    as they follow his Covenant ways
    and remember to do whatever he said.

God has set his throne in heaven;
  he rules over us all. He's the King!
So bless God, you angels,
  ready and able to fly at his bidding,
  quick to hear and do what he says.
Bless God, all you armies of angels,
  alert to respond to whatever he wills.
Bless God, all creatures, wherever you are—
  everything and everyone made by God.

And you, O my soul, bless God!
Psalm 103 *The Message*

• • •

Praise be to the God and Father of our Lord Jesus Christ! In his great mercy he has given us new birth into a living hope through the resurrection of Jesus Christ from the dead, and into an inheritance that can never perish, spoil or fade. This inheritance is kept in heaven for you, who through faith are shielded by God's power until the coming of the salvation that is ready to be revealed in the last time. In all this you greatly rejoice, though now for a little while you may have had to suffer grief in all kinds of trials. These have come so that your faith—of greater worth than gold, which perishes even though refined by fire—may be proved genuine and may result in praise, glory and honor when Jesus Christ is revealed. Though you have not seen him, you love him; and even though you do not see him now, you believe in him and are filled with an inexpressible and glorious joy, for you are receiving the end result of your faith, the salvation of your souls.

1 Peter 1:3-9 niv

• • •

Others

1 Chronicles 29:10-13

Psalm 28:6-9

Psalm 30

Psalm 100

Psalm 145

Psalm 150

Guilt

> Have mercy on me, O God,
> 　according to your steadfast love;
> according to your abundant mercy
> 　blot out my transgressions.
> Wash me thoroughly from my iniquity,
> 　and cleanse me from my sin.
>
> For I know my transgressions,
> 　and my sin is ever before me.
> Against you, you alone, have I sinned,
> 　and done what is evil in your sight,
> so that you are justified in your sentence
> 　and blameless when you pass judgment. . . .
>
> Purge me with hyssop, and I shall be clean;
> 　wash me, and I shall be whiter than snow.
> Let me hear joy and gladness;
> 　let the bones that you have crushed rejoice.
> Hide your face from my sins,

and blot out all my iniquities.
Create in me a clean heart, O God,
    and put a new and right spirit within me.
Do not cast me away from your presence,
    and do not take your holy spirit from me.
Restore to me the joy of your salvation,
    and sustain in me a willing spirit.
Then I will teach transgressors your ways,
    and sinners will return to you. . . .
The sacrifice acceptable to God is a broken
        spirit;
    a broken and contrite heart, O God, you will
        not despise.

PSALM 51:1-4, 7-13, 17 NRSV

•   •   •

Generous in love—God, give grace!
Huge in mercy—wipe out my bad record.
Scrub away my guilt,
    soak out my sins in your laundry.
I know how bad I've been;
    my sins are staring me down.

You're the One I've violated, and you've seen
    it all, seen the full extent of my evil.
You have all the facts before you;
    whatever you decide about me is fair. . . .
Soak me in your laundry and I'll come out clean,
    scrub me and I'll have a snow-white life.

Tune me in to foot-tapping songs,
    set these once-broken bones to dancing.
Don't look too close for blemishes,
    give me a clean bill of health.
God, make a fresh start in me,
    shape a Genesis week from the chaos of my life.
Don't throw me out with the trash,
    or fail to breathe holiness in me.
Bring me back from gray exile,
    put a fresh wind in my sails!
Give me a job teaching rebels your ways
    so the lost can find their way home. . . .
I learned God-worship
    when my pride was shattered.
Heart-shattered lives ready for love
    don't for a moment escape God's notice.
PSALM 51:1-4, 7-13, 17 *The Message*

• • •

Hear me, LORD, and answer me,
    for I am poor and needy.
Guard my life, for I am faithful to you;
    save your servant who trusts in you.
You are my God; have mercy on me, Lord,
    for I call to you all day long.
Bring joy to your servant, Lord,
    for I put my trust in you.

You, Lord, are forgiving and good,

abounding in love to all who call to you.
Hear my prayer, LORD;
    listen to my cry for mercy.
When I am in distress, I call to you,
    because you answer me.

Teach me your way, LORD,
    that I may rely on your faithfulness;
give me an undivided heart,
    that I may fear your name.
I will praise you, Lord my God, with all my heart;
    I will glorify your name forever.
For great is your love toward me;
    you have delivered me from the depths,
    from the realm of the dead.

Arrogant foes are attacking me, O God;
    a band of ruthless people seeks my life—
    they have no regard for you.
But you, Lord, are a compassionate and
       gracious God,
    slow to anger, abounding in love and
       faithfulness.
Turn to me and have mercy on me;
    show your strength in behalf of your servant
save me, because I serve you
    just as my mother did.
Give me a sign of your goodness,

> that my enemies may see it and be put to shame,
>> for you, LORD, have helped me and
>> comforted me.

PSALM 86:1-7, 11-17 NIV

• • •

I ask you, therefore, not to be discouraged because of my sufferings for you, which are your glory.

For this reason I kneel before the Father, from whom every family in heaven and on earth derives its name. I pray that out of his glorious riches he may strengthen you with power through his Spirit in your inner being, so that Christ may dwell in your hearts through faith. And I pray that you, being rooted and established in love, may have power, together with all the Lord's holy people, to grasp how wide and long and high and deep is the love of Christ, and to know this love that surpasses knowledge—that you may be filled to the measure of all the fullness of God.

Now to him who is able to do immeasurably more than all we ask or imagine, according to his power that is at work within us, to him be glory in the church and in Christ Jesus throughout all generations, for ever and ever! Amen.

EPHESIANS 3:13-21 NIV

• • •

Others

Psalm 25

Psalm 32

Psalm 139:1-17, 23-24

Isaiah 1:18

Isaiah 53

Matthew 9:2-8

John 3:16-21

Romans 5:1-11

1 John 1:1-9

1 John 4:9-21

Loneliness

You have searched me, LORD,
   and you know me.
You know when I sit and when I rise;
   you perceive my thoughts from afar.
You discern my going out and my lying down;
   you are familiar with all my ways.
Before a word is on my tongue
   you, LORD, know it completely.
You hem me in behind and before,
   and you lay your hand upon me.
Such knowledge is too wonderful for me,
   too lofty for me to attain.

Where can I go from your Spirit?
    Where can I flee from your presence?
PSALM 139:1-7 NIV

. . .

Trust in the LORD with all your heart,
    and do not rely on your own insight.
In all your ways acknowledge him,
    and he will make straight your paths.
PROVERBS 3:5-6 NRSV

. . .

Trust GOD from the bottom of your heart;
    Don't try to figure out everything on your
        own.
Listen for GOD'S voice in everything you do,
        everywhere you go;
    He's the one who will keep you on track.
PROVERBS 3:5-6 *The Message*

. . .

Therefore, since we are justified by faith, we have
peace with God through our Lord Jesus Christ, through
whom we have obtained access to this grace in which
we stand; and we boast in our hope of sharing the glory
of God. And not only that, but we also boast in our sufferings, knowing that suffering produces endurance,
and endurance produces character, and character produces hope, and hope does not disappoint us, because

God's love has been poured into our hearts through the Holy Spirit that has been given to us.

ROMANS 5:1-5 NRSV

· · ·

By entering through faith into what God has always wanted to do for us—set us right with him, make us fit for him—we have it all together with God because of our Master Jesus. And that's not all: We throw open our doors to God and discover at the same moment that he has already thrown open his door to us. We find ourselves standing where we always hoped we might stand—out in the wide open spaces of God's grace and glory, standing tall and shouting our praise.

There's more to come: We continue to shout our praise even when we're hemmed in with troubles, because we know how troubles can develop passionate patience in us, and how that patience in turn forges the tempered steel of virtue, keeping us alert for whatever God will do next. In alert expectancy such as this, we're never left feeling shortchanged. Quite the contrary—we can't round up enough containers to hold everything God generously pours into our lives through the Holy Spirit!

ROMANS 5:1-5 *The Message*

· · ·

This is the confidence we have in approaching God: that if we ask anything according to his will, he hears us. And if we know that he hears us—whatever we ask—we know that we have what we asked of him.

1 JOHN 5:14-15 NIV

• • •

Others

Isaiah 49:13-15

Matthew 28:20

John 14:1-6

John 15:7-11

Philippians 4:4-7

Hebrews 12:1-2

1 Peter 1:3-9

Sickness

Whoever dwells in the shelter of the Most High
   will rest in the shadow of the Almighty.
They say of the Lord, "He is my refuge and
      my fortress,
   my God, in whom I trust."

Surely he will save you from the fowler's snare
   and from the deadly pestilence.
He will cover you with his feathers,

and under his wings you will find refuge;
his faithfulness will be your shield and
rampart.
You will not fear the terror of night,
nor the arrow that flies by day,
nor the pestilence that stalks in the darkness,
nor the plague that destroys at midday.
"Because he loves me," says the LORD, "I will
rescue him;
I will protect him, for he acknowledges my
name.
He will call on me, and I will answer him;
I will be with him in trouble,
I will deliver him and honor him.
With long life I will satisfy him
and show him my salvation."

PSALM 91:1-6, 14-16 NIV

• • •

I lift up my eyes to the hills—
from where will my help come?
My help comes from the LORD,
who made heaven and earth.

He will not let your foot be moved;
he who keeps you will not slumber.
He who keeps Israel
will neither slumber nor sleep.

The LORD is your keeper;
    the LORD is your shade at your right hand.
The sun shall not strike you by day,
    nor the moon by night.
The Lord will keep you from all evil;
    he will keep your life.
The Lord will keep your going out and your
      coming in
    from this time on and forevermore.
PSALM 121 NRSV

· · ·

I look up to the mountains;
    does my strength come from mountains?
No, my strength comes from GOD,
    who made heaven, and earth, and
      mountains.

He won't let you stumble,
    your Guardian God won't fall asleep.
Not on your life! Israel's
    Guardian will never doze or sleep.

GOD'S your Guardian,
    right at your side to protect you—
Shielding you from sunstroke,
    sheltering you from moonstroke.

GOD guards you from every evil,
    he guards your very life.

He guards you when you leave and when you
     return,
  he guards you now, he guards you always.
PSALM 121 *The Message*

· · ·

Others

Matthew 8:1-13

Matthew 9:2-8, 18-26

Matthew 11:28-30

Matthew 15:21-28

Luke 4:38-44

Luke 6:6-10

Luke 17:11-19

John 4:46-53

John 14:27

Romans 8:38-39

James 5:10-20

Celebration

LORD, our Lord,
  how majestic is your name in all the earth!

You have set your glory
  in the heavens.
Through the praise of children and infants

you have established a stronghold against
 your enemies,
to silence the foe and the avenger.

When I consider your heavens, the work of
 your fingers,
 the moon and the stars, which you have set
 in place,
what are mere mortals that you are mindful of
 them,
 human beings that you care for them?

You have made them a little lower than the
 angels
 and crowned them with glory and honor.
You made them rulers over the works of your
 hands;
 you put everything under their feet:
all flocks and herds,
 and the animals of the wild,
the birds in the sky,
 and the fish in the sea,
 all that swim the paths of the seas.

LORD, our Lord,
 how majestic is your name in all the earth!
PSALM 8 NIV

• • •

Make a joyful noise to the LORD, all the earth.
    Worship the LORD with gladness;
    come into his presence with singing.

Know that the LORD is God.
    It is he that made us, and we are his;
    we are his people, and the sheep of his pasture.

Enter his gates with thanksgiving,
    and his courts with praise.
    Give thanks to him, bless his name.

For the LORD is good;
    his steadfast love endures forever,
    and his faithfulness to all generations.

PSALM 100 NRSV

• • •

On your feet now—applaud GOD! Bring a gift
        of laughter,
    sing yourselves into his presence.

Know this: GOD is God, and God, GOD.
    He made us; we didn't make him.
    We're his people, his well-tended sheep.

Enter with the password: "Thank you!"
    Make yourselves at home, talking praise.
    Thank him. Worship him.

For GOD is sheer beauty,

all-generous in love,
loyal always and ever.
PSALM 100 *The Message*

. . .

I will extol you, my God and King,
and bless your name forever and ever.
Every day I will bless you,
and praise your name forever and ever.
Great is the LORD, and greatly to be praised;
his greatness is unsearchable. . . .

The LORD is gracious and merciful,
slow to anger and abounding in steadfast
love.
The LORD is good to all,
and his compassion is over all that he
has made. . . .

The LORD is just in all his ways,
and kind in all his doings.
The LORD is near to all who call on him,
to all who call on him in truth.
He fulfills the desire of all who fear him;
he also hears their cry, and saves them.
PSALM 145:1-3, 8-9, 17-19 NRSV

. . .

I lift you high in praise, my God, O my King!
and I'll bless your name into eternity.

I'll bless you every day,
  and keep it up from now to eternity.
GOD is magnificent; he can never be praised
      enough.
  There are no boundaries to his greatness. . . .

GOD is all mercy and grace—
  not quick to anger, is rich in love.

GOD is good to one and all;
  everything he does is suffused with grace. . . .

Everything GOD does is right—
  the trademark on all his works is love.

GOD's there, listening for all who pray,
  for all who pray and mean it.

He does what's best for those who fear him—
  hears them call out, and saves them. . . .
PSALM 145:1-3, 8-9, 17-19 *The Message*

• • •

If God is for us, who can be against us? He who did
not spare his own Son, but gave him up for us all—
how will he not also, along with him, graciously give
us all things? Who will bring any charge against those
whom God has chosen? It is God who justifies. Who
then is the one who condemns? No one. Christ Jesus
who died—more than that, who was raised to life—is

at the right hand of God and is also interceding for us. Who shall separate us from the love of Christ? Shall trouble or hardship or persecution or famine or nakedness or danger or sword? As it is written:

> "For your sake we face death all day long;
> we are considered as sheep to be slaughtered."

No, in all these things we are more than conquerors through him who loved us. For I am convinced that neither death nor life, neither angels nor demons, neither the present nor the future, nor any powers, neither height nor depth, nor anything else in all creation, will be able to separate us from the love of God that is in Christ Jesus our Lord.

ROMANS 8:31-39 NIV

• • •

Others

Matthew 12:22-31

Romans 5:1-11

Notes

page 21   "O Ingenious God": Ted Loder, "Touch Me Deeply so That I Will Find a Sense of Self," in *Before the Amen: Creative Resources for Worship,* ed. Maren C. Tirabassi and Maria I. Tirabassi (Cleveland, Ohio: Pilgrim, 2007), p. 82.

page 22   "Gentle me": Ted Loder, "Guide Me into an Unclenched Moment," in *Guerrillas of Grace: Prayers for the Battle* (San Diego: LuraMedia, 1984), p. 17.

page 22   "Eternal Friend": Ted Loder, "I Need to Breathe Deeply," in *Guerillas of Grace,* pp. 22-23.

page 24   "O Eternal One": Ted Loder, "It Would Be Easier to Pray if I Were Clear," in *Before the Amen*, ed. Tirabassi and Tirabassi, p. 26.

page 25   "O God of children": Ted Loder, "Grant Me an Enchantment of Heart," in *Before the Amen*, ed. Tirabassi and Tirabassi, p. 27.

page 29   "When grief is raw": Brian Wren, "When Grief Is Raw," in *The Covenant Hymnal: A Worshipbook* (Chicago: Covenant, 1996), p. 461.

page 47   "God of all knowledge": Sheryl Stewart, under the heading "Learning Disorders," in *Before the Amen*, ed. Tirabassi and Tirabassi, p. 224.

page 66   "Gracious God": Sue Henley, under the heading "Divorce, Marriage, Changing

	Churches," in *Before the Amen*, ed. Tirabassi and Tirabassi, p. 177.
page 94	"All may gather": Adapted from F. Russell Mitman, *Blessed by the Presence of God: Liturgies for Occasional Services* (Cleveland, Ohio: Pilgrim, 2007), pp. 123-27.
page 101	"Loving God": Glen E. Rainsley, *Hear Our Prayer* (Cleveland, Ohio: United Church Press, 1996).
page 121	"We give thanks": Sue Henley, "We Give Thanks for an Ordinary Day," in *Before the Amen*, ed. Tirabassi and Tirabassi, p. 208.
page 146	"It's a brand new day": Marilee Zdenek, *God Is a Verb!* (Waco, Tex.: Word Books, 1974), p. 91.
page 150	"The wind of the Spirit": Ibid., p. 88.